Sons of Scotland

A Family Story of
Brothers from The Gorbals

Joseph Hughes GC. RASC and James Hughes RN

Best Wishes Lesley Goad
01-08-2018

Lesley Goad

"In Life we don't remember days,

We remember moments"

Cesare Pavese 1908-1950

First published by Milton Contact Ltd

ISBN: 978-1-911526-25-4

Milton Contact Ltd
3, Hall End, Milton, Cambridge, UK.
CB24 6AQ
www.miltoncontact.co.uk

milton ContacT

Song for the Sons of Scotland

Joseph Hughes 1926-1946 James Hughes 1924-

Sons of Scotland were sent far to roam
In a war-torn world, one never more to come home.
Sons of Scotland, brothers with their worlds torn apart,
But their Scottish Homeland's always safe in their hearts.

Chorus:
Two Glasgow brothers called to serve their King
And in their praise we all will sing.

Sailor James was called for the seas to roam,
But safely returned to his dear Scottish home.
Four years of conflict, which took him far and wide.
In HMS Pheasant, he sailed every war-torn tide.

Repeat Chorus

Now in times of peace 'Fate' took James far away.
In the heart of a great continent he decided to stay.
He married and raised a family in Australia grand,
Now an adopted son of this 'New Promised Land'.

Repeat Chorus

Soldier Joseph was sent to far eastern lands to roam,
But sadly, young Joseph, was never more to come home.
His cheeky smile and joy of youth, to end in sacrifice;
With a brave feat of valour, in which he gave his life.

Repeat Chorus

King and Country gave thanks and presented a George Cross,
The pride of his Regiment, also helped comfort a family's loss.
Hong Kong 's grateful people laid him in a place of their own,
Now he sleeps, not forgotten, in a chosen foreign home.

Repeat Chorus

Sons of Scotland were sent far to roam
In a war-torn world, one never more to come home.
Sons of Scotland, brothers with their worlds torn apart,
But their Scottish homeland's always safe in their hearts.

Chorus:
Two Glasgow brothers called to serve their King
And in their praise we all will sing.

Lesley Goad

Dedication

'A Devoted Cousin'

CATHERINE HUGHES-FINN

(IRENE)

1937-2016

Also remembering her husband

Thomas Finn (Tommy)

1935-2015

Contents

Bill Goad and Sally Hughes Wedding, 1943

Tom and Ida Goad, Dan Malone, Bill and Sally, Mollie Goad John and Sarah Hughes

Introduction

'Putting You in The Picture'

The above words were so often used, when reminiscing with our father, William Goad. He was a man of great curiosity about everything in life and, if fate had not taken him to Scotland and he had not married Sarah Hughes, from the Gorbals, Glasgow, in 1943, then this amazing family story would never have been written.

Consequently today, we have discovered a large family of Scottish and Australian cousins, who can be added to our immediate family. Coincidentally, like his brother-in-law, Joseph Hughes GC, Bill Goad was also to end his wartime service being the proud holder of the George Cross. But that is another story to be found in my 'Fen Farming Family'. This book is its sequel.

This picture I am creating for you to-day is of our mother Sarah's two younger brothers, James Hughes RN and Joseph Hughes GC and also of their young cousin, Irene Hughes-Finn.

This is their special story, a picture with all its shades of dark and light, which I, as Bill and Sally's daughter-in-law, will paint for you with my pen.

All were born and bred in the Gorbals district of Glasgow of a large Irish/Scottish family, during the austere time of the great depression between the two world wars of the twentieth century.

As young men, both James and Joseph were called to serve their King and country at the time of WWII.

Seventy years later their cousin Irene's memories and actions were to influence the writing of this book. This family story begins in 1939 during the dark days of impending war with Adolf Hitler's Germany.

As a seventeen-year-old boy sailor, Bill Goad was a gunner on one of the Tribal Class Destroyers, HMS Mashona, deployed on convoy in the Arctic from a base at Scapa Flow, which regularly docked for repairs at Greenock, Scotland.

Welcome shore leave was spent in the nearby City of Glasgow, giving a much-needed break from the battles of war and the rigorous discipline on board ship.

One fateful day he happened to meet a pretty brown eyed, dark haired Scottish lass called Sarah (always known as Sally) Hughes, a local girl from the Gorbals district of the City and, as in all good stories, they fell in love.

Four years later, in 1943, they were married and she made her home in England, at Hill Farm, Stretham, Cambridgeshire, Bill Goad's family home. Bill, by then a Petty Officer, was still away fighting the enemy at sea.

Sally was the eldest and only daughter of John and Sarah Hughes's four children, who with her three brothers, James, Joseph and Francis, lived in one of the large tenement housing blocks at 159, Pollockshaws Road, in the Gorbals district of Glasgow.

James enlisted as soon as he was eighteen in 1942, and spent four wartime years at sea, serving in the Royal Navy, travelling the world, taking part in many theatres of war. He was then demobbed to be safely back home in Glasgow, in March 1946.

Joseph, at eighteen in the September of 1944, chose to join the Royal Army Service Corps as a driver. In March 1946, whilst serving in Hong Kong with the RASC, and still only nineteen, he tragically died as a result of an explosion.

James and Joseph, both young men were really not much more than boys, but they had lives full of adventure and courage. Their stories so different, but, some seventy years later, they were to unite the Hughes and Goad families across time and worlds. They were also to inspire the writing of this book in 2017.

By 1949, James was still living in Glasgow, but due to his personal family circumstances, he made the decision to emigrate to Australia to build himself a new life.

He then visited his sister Sally and family in Stretham, Cambridgeshire to say farewell before leaving. James and Sally corresponded until her death in 1988, after which both families – the Hughes and the Goads – lost touch.

No more letters were exchanged by the next generations, as, sadly, their grandparents passed away in the 1960s and Sally Goad's youngest brother, Frank Hughes had also died in 1981. There was now only Uncle James left of the little Pollockshaws Road family, with him now living so far away in Australia.

Meanwhile, in the City of Glasgow, Sally's young cousin, Irene Hughes, had now grown up and was married to Tommy Finn.

Unknown to us at our home in Cambridgeshire, she had spent many years campaigning in her home city, to get its recognition for Joseph Hughes's courageous action in Hong Kong. After which, his country had posthumously awarded him the George Cross, in which his family took enormous pride.

Eventually, in March 2006, on the sixtieth anniversary of his death, a Memorial was finally placed in Glasgow, in the Gorbals at St Francis Community Centre, Cumberland Street. It was a proud day for Irene and the Scottish Hughes family.

And thanks to Irene's efforts, all were there honouring him as a 'Son of the City'. Paddy and I attended that day, but we didn't meet Irene or even know of her role in the day's events.

In 2014, I as the wife of Bill and Sally Goad's son, Paddy, wrote and published the book 'Fen Farming Family'. It was the story of my search for the Goad farming ancestors.

As a result, the world-wide web opened the door to my writing, leading on to the conception and birth of this sequel book and the creation of my story today.

First of all, in 2015, I received an e-mail via Ancestry from a cousin in Australia. Uncle James's Hughes family there were looking for us all. His younger Hughes generation were getting curious as to their heritage. The wonders of modern technology and my book writing had worked their magic and had connected us across the world as a family again.

For a few months Paddy and I corresponded and talked by phone to Uncle James, a healthy 90-year-old living in Queensland, and in no time we decided that we must pay him a visit.

Now was the time, therefore, to gather more information about our Scottish Hughes family, on behalf of their long-lost relative, James, so that we could take it out to Australia with us.

Fate lent us a hand here. For, having been at Joseph's Memorial tribute in Glasgow in 2006, we managed to obtained cousin Irene's telephone number and so began our new contact with our unknown cousin in Scotland, getting to know her through talking and exchanging letters.

In 'Fen Farming Family' I had written an account of Joseph's heroic action and so I sent Irene a copy of my book for her interest. A few weeks later, after she had read it, a large package arrived for me in the post, enclosing her many years of campaigning letters she had written and received in her quest for a memorial in Glasgow for Joseph. She also enclosed a note, asking me if I would be her "Book Angel" and urging me to "fulfil her lifelong wish, to have Joseph's story written for all to know."

The need for Joseph's story to be told for the family appealed to me, as I had already done a basic research of events for my first book and his three Goad nephews were also very proud of his sacrifice and memory. After thinking it through, I wrote to Irene and agreed to be her "Book Angel" and to try and do justice to her request.

We had booked to fly out to Australia in March 2016. By coincidence, March 2016 was the 70th anniversary of Joseph's heroic action in Hong Kong, so we stopped off there for three days on the way. With the help of Joseph's regiment, the Royal Army Service Corps, now renamed as the Royal Logistic Corps, who are based at Deepcut Barracks, Surrey, and the Hong Kong Royal British Legion, it was arranged for us to visit and to lay flowers at his grave, on behalf of cousin Irene and Uncle James and also to pay our own respects.

By now I had begun to realise what a great story I had found.

Next, it was onto Australia to meet Uncle James, our two cousins, Malcolm and Christine, and their extended families, all living in North Queensland. So, the sequel to 'Fen Farming Family' had begun!

On first meeting, we instantly felt the family bond and spent many happy hours talking about his interesting years of life in Australia.

I heard of the contrasting lives of the two brothers, and all this seemed to connect in my mind, re-enforcing my idea of the book 'Sons of Scotland'.

Happily, Uncle James gave it his blessing and became keen to be a part of my project. He began to reminisce, giving lively and interesting accounts of his many Antipodean tales of over 60 years. And relating his many adventures as a colonial immigrant in the austere years following WWII.

It has been a pleasure for Paddy and I to get to know all our 'long-lost' Scottish and Australian families, but sadly, in September 2016, cousin Irene (Hughes) Finn, who had done so much to keep the memory of Joseph alive, passed away. But the story of her long, successful quest will be told, as she was the real catalyst for this book.

Although she only saw my writing at the planning stage, she will have died happy, knowing that her dream was at last being fulfilled. Her love for her cousin Josie will be part of her immortality.

There are three extraordinary stories here: Irene's was one such and those of the brothers, Joseph and James, were even more so, perhaps. I sincerely hope I have done them all justice.

I am sure the guiding hand of fate has touched us all, working to reunite a family. And enabling me to 'put you in the picture' about two special brothers, both of whose lives were touched by war, and about another major character in our story, a younger female cousin. It is also thanks to her that, all of seventy years later, we have a number of stories, which contribute to the renewal of family bonds across the world.

On a more personal note, through our joint efforts, this big, new picture of the Hughes family of Glasgow has made it possible for me to tell of the very interesting impact it has had on all our lives.

In conclusion, I hope that readers will enjoy following the different threads I have woven. And sharing with us all the highs and lows of these remarkable people, who have touched my life and whom I have been very pleased to bring together in this book.

Lesley Goad 2017

Chapter One

The City of Glasgow and the Hughes Family

'Let Glasgow Flourish'

Glasgow City Hall

Irene placing a tribute to Joseph Hughes GC.
George Square Garden of Remembrance, Glasgow

'The City of Glasgow and the Hughes Family'

Glasgow is the second city of Scotland and twice the size of its capital, Edinburgh. But it was always an important city. Its ancient University was founded in 1481, being the fourth oldest in the English-speaking world. Owing to the development of its great shipping and industrial might in the 18th century, it then proudly became known as the 'Second City of the British Empire' across the world.

By the end of the 19th century its population had increased five-fold, all working together, helping to create this great city of wealth. In the true spirit of the city's motto 'Let Glasgow Flourish': a phrase taken from a sermon of the city's founder and patron saint, St. Mungo.

By the turn of the 20th century it could now proudly display the signs of its success, with large green parks for Sunday recreation, fine classical buildings: libraries, art galleries, banks and numerous imposing department stores in its wide, new streets, all for the delight of its hard-working, thriving population.

All this was crowned by the grand and imposing City Hall building, newly completed in 1883 in the large city centre, overlooking George Square, which contains the people's memorial of the 'Garden of Remembrance'.

Along with its docks and ship building on the River Clyde, it was the largest seaport in Britain, the Firth of Clyde becoming known as the 'Gateway to the Americas' with its prosperous trade of tobacco and sugar.

All this expansion of industries over the years attracted a newly needed workforce from across the surrounding countryside and especially large numbers coming across the water from rural

Ireland. As the census tells us in the 1850s, 18% of Glasgow's population had emigrated to escape the scourge of the potato famine.

In the 1870s George Hughes and his wife, Catherine, with their family of six children, arrived from Tulliallen, Co. Louth, in Ireland, to make a new life in Glasgow. George traded as a coal merchant, in a much-needed occupation, as local Scottish coal was the driving fuel of the city's industrial revolution.

In 1875, George and Catherine's last and only Scots-born child, a daughter, Catherine, was born at their home in 181, Pollockshaws Road, in the Gorbals district. It was only in 1846 that the Gorbals district had become part of the City of Glasgow.

This ancient area, just south of the River Clyde, and once church land, had previously been the site of the old leper hospital, established in 1350, which was still in use in 1610. It had received alms by royalty and 'the great and the good'.

By the late 1900s, the Gorbals consisted of a multitude of streets, built with tenement blocks of crowded housing. This area grew with the influx of the newly arrived Irish Catholic workers, who were mostly employed in the local heavy industries, all living together as a close community, helping each other in the populous bustle of life.

George and Catherine's youngest Irish-born son, John, born in 1873, was just a baby when they arrived in Glasgow, and when he was old enough, he worked in the local iron foundry. In 1896, he married Catherine Herd, of nearby Salisbury Street, Gorbals, at St. John's Roman Catholic Church in Portugal Street, Gorbals. They lived at 40, Denmore Street, Gorbals, where their first child, a son also called John, was born in 1897. This John Hughes was one day destined to become the father of brothers, James Hughes RN and Joseph Hughes GC, our two 'Sons of Scotland'.

In the 1911 census, young John Hughes was 14, living at home and working as a labourer. He had six siblings, but, importantly, his young brother, Charles, just aged 2, born in 1909 at 4, Thistle Street, was also destined to become the father of our cousin, Catherine (Irene) Hughes-Finn, who is also to feature largely in this story.

John and his brother, Charles, were both first generation Scots, born into their Irish immigrant family. In 1916, on the birth certificate of their youngest brother, James, the family was now living at 3, Francis Street, and their father, John, was recorded as being a Private in 4th Battalion, Scottish Rifles. Surprisingly, at 43 years of age, he was still serving his country in WWI.

His eldest son, John, now eighteen in 1916, was also called to fight, joining the Royal Artillery. This was the year of compulsory conscription, which was needed in view of the shocking tragic losses of the Battle of the Somme that summer.

There is a lovely photograph of him in uniform and written on the back is 'John in France on his horse, Billy'.

Grandfather John Hughes on his horse, Billy
in the uniform of the Royal Artillery

Since the Hughes were a family of carters, working with horses would have been second nature to John. Luckily, both father and son were to return safely to the family at the end of the war. Upon demobilisation, young John continued to work as a carter of coal in the family business. The big city railway coal yards were conveniently located adjacent to Pollockshaws Road, where he was later to make his home, when, on September 26th 1919, he married Sarah Wogan in Hutchesontown, Gorbals.

Sarah was an Irish Catholic girl from Dublin, whose father, Christopher Wogan, was a hairdresser by trade. He and his family had left Dublin in the Spring of 1916, then a city in turmoil after the violent Republican 'Easter Risings'.

He had been hoping to begin a safer, new life with his family in Glasgow, only to find himself, after his journey across the choppy Irish Sea, under arrest, as they disembarked from the ferry.

The Scottish police were suspicious of him owing to his religion, his nationality and the timing of his arrival. He was thoroughly investigated before being allowed to stay. Life was difficult for peaceful Irish Catholics at this time of national war and, especially, during Ireland's political uprisings.

John and Sarah Hughes lived in one of the many workers' tenements, home being on the first floor at 159, Pollockshaws Road. Their first surviving child was a daughter, Sarah, born October 29th 1922, whom they named after her mother, but, thereafter, she was always known as Sally.

A son, James, was born August 2nd 1924 and another son, Joseph, on September 1st 1926. To complete their family, a son Francis, was born on December 13th 1927.

The four siblings were all to become pupils at St. John's R.C. School and as a family, they attended the nearby St. John's R.C. Church in Portugal Street each Sunday, and afterwards they always went for a family gathering at the home of their grandparents, John and Catherine Hughes, in Denmore Street.

All would be dressed in their black 'Sunday Best' for going to Mass at St. John's. Men in their suits, ladies and girls in smart dresses, boys in their traditional sailor suits and shiny black shoes, all ready and excited, waiting to be given their Sunday 'Penny' by their grandfather, John, and tea by grandmother Catherine.

In the 1930s, the younger John Hughes began working for the Railways, and was to ultimately become an Inspector with them. Paddy Goad has the memory of when, on holiday with his grandparents in Glasgow as a young boy, he went with grandfather John to his office, situated in the big coal-black, dusty railway yard behind the tenements. He remembers feeling so proud that his granddad had an office!

This visit created a lasting impression on him of Glasgow at that time. The memories of it are still very much with him today.

First, of climbing the many stairs in the tenements and admiring the brightly polished brass named door-plates, especially the one opposite on their landing, saying 'Mr Findlay', of being much impressed when his grandmother told him he was an engine driver.

A memory then, of going down to the busy street to visit the community bath-house with her. It was all such a contrast with the green Cambridgeshire countryside, where he lived, and with his other grandfather's familiar farm, where he spent so much of his time as a boy.

In conclusion, therefore, John and his five Hughes brothers, George, Thomas, Joseph, Charles, James and their sister Mary Anne, were all first-generation Scots of Irish descent. They were raised, lived and worked in Glasgow, as it evolved during their life-time.

Most of the family's descendants live there still. And all of them are proud Glaswegians, who have made their own mark, playing their individual part in the development of a successful modern city.

A city which has now honoured its son, Joseph Hughes, GC in many ways, after all the years his cousin, Irene, had strived for local recognition for his heroic action in Hong Kong. Both their stories are recorded in this book and also, the fascinating story of his elder brother, James Hughes.

Each brother courageously serving his country in wartime, one with great heroism. And with James, who survives to this day, we have a true Scottish story of an emigrant life of achievements, spanning many years in another land, but throughout, always carrying his Scottish heritage close to his heart.

John and Sarah Hughes

The armorial insignia of the City of Glasgow,
based on the legends of the city's patron saint, St. Mungo.
With permission of The Lord Lyons Office

Chapter Two

Joseph's Story – 'The Hero of Kowloon'

Joseph Hughes GC. RASC

1926-1946

Joseph sitting on his army truck
Hong Kong, Christmas Day, 1945

The Story of Joseph Hughes GC.

Joseph's birth was registered by his father, John Hughes, a carter, on September 6th in the City of Glasgow. In fact, he had been born September 1st 1926, at 5.45pm, at 29, Falfield Street, Glasgow.

Maybe they hadn't yet moved to 159, Pollockshaws Road, Gorbals, the familiar family address we all know of later! Or perhaps Sarah had gone home to her mother to give birth, as was so often done in this uncertain era of childbirth in the 1920s of high infant mortality. One of its causes being 'bad milk', containing unspecified additives to give bulk. This is one of Uncle James's childhood memories and what he was told, after losing his baby sister, Christine. Then, only the most robust babies survived infancy.

Joseph was John and Sarah's second born son, his brother, James (Jimmy), being the elder, and his sister, Sarah (Sally), was the oldest of them all. Just a year later in 1927, Francis (Frank) was born to complete this little family.

They were all christened in St. John's RC Church on Portugal Street and, when aged five, all attended the St. John's School, until they were fourteen years of age.

All were clever children, the two youngest, Joe and Frank, loved playing football and the home was always full of singing and music. Life was happy for the little loving family.

When he was old enough, Joe enjoyed helping his father, John, deliver coal. The previous three generations of Hughes men were also known to have been connected with coal deliveries in the City of Glasgow. His father, John, later joined the Railway, working in the local goods yards behind their large tenement building home on Pollockshaws Road, where he was eventually to obtain the position of Inspector.

But as a young teenager, his elder brother James remembers, when school was out, Joe locally delivered coal briquettes with a hand-built trolley, accompanied on his rounds by his little terrier. He could be heard whistling and singing as he pulled his cart around the Gorbals busy streets. Joe would often call in and see his Uncle Charlie and Aunt Esther in Camden Street and tease his young cousin, Irene, whose special name for him was 'Josie'. She would love to play with his little dog, Trixie, who always trotted at Joe's heels with her jaunty tail in the air.

As soon as he was old enough, Joe learnt to drive a lorry and got a job as a delivery driver for the local coal merchant J. J. Vernal, of Pollockshaws. This was the district of the railway goods yards, storing the vast tons of coal delivered from Scottish pits, which heated Glasgow's homes and fuelled their industries, creating at this time the accustomed smoke and dust in the air, which coated the tenement homes of its population with its sooty grime.

In the summer evenings, Joe and his friends met in these bustling, close-knit streets of the Gorbals, laughing, playing football and, sometimes, they would have a sing-song of a popular music hall ditty, with Joe happily strumming on his banjo.

One evening, at the entrance of his close, Joe and his pals were ticked off by the local 'bobby' for the noise they were making in their fun, but, as always, he left them with a smile on his face at the cheery banter of the happy young lads. This a memory of his cousin, Irene.

There was no special girl in his life for Joe at this time. His friend, Ian Cameron, remembers that for evening entertainment they went to The Taxi Dancing, where you bought tickets to dance with the local girls – a kind of dance-hall, originating in the US and “all very proper” actually.

But it was now the days of WWII and Glasgow had been badly bombed in the blitz of the early 1940s. Its large areas of heavy industry and shipyards were an important target for the German Luftwaffe. In the June of 1944, there had been the amazing joint forces effort of the Normandy invasion of German occupied France, and now the tide of war was beginning to turn in the Allied forces favour.

In September of that year, Joseph was to become eighteen and, as all young men were still needed to serve their country, so Joe was called up to become part of the Royal Army Service Corps. Happily, at this time, two of his Gorbals pals joined with him in this new life, Ian Cameron and Donald Williams. Together with Joe's younger brother, Frank, now aged 16, they had their photographs taken together in Glasgow before leaving.

Joe's love of driving and skills as a driver held him in good stead and he was sent for army training in Lancashire, England. He was now to be known as Private J. Hughes, No. 14858103, and was training at Squiresgate Camp, 9th Kings PTC, Lytham St. Annes.

Ian Cameron-Joseph-Donald Williams- Brother Frank

Joe in uniform

Joseph with friend

It was 12th November 1944, when, on a day's leave visiting the Central Promenade in nearby Blackpool, proudly wearing his new uniform, he had his first photograph taken especially to send to his mother and father back home.

This was a new life in a new world for an 18-year-old boy, who had never left his home city of Glasgow. Joseph was following in the footsteps of his brother James, stepping out into the world of wartime conflict, the fate of so many young men of his time, leaving home to do their duty to defend their country.

At Christmas 1944, he sent a card to his sister, Sally, which we still have. It has the regimental badge on it with just a few written words. "From Joe. To Sally, Bill and Baby" – his nephew, Christopher, just 8 months old.

The card was posted from Sheffield, England, but addressed to Pollockshaws Road, since, that Christmas, his sister, Sally, had gone home to her parents for the festivities, as her husband, Bill, was still away at sea.

Joe finished the address with the words BONNIE SCOTLAND. Missing home a little bit, was he?

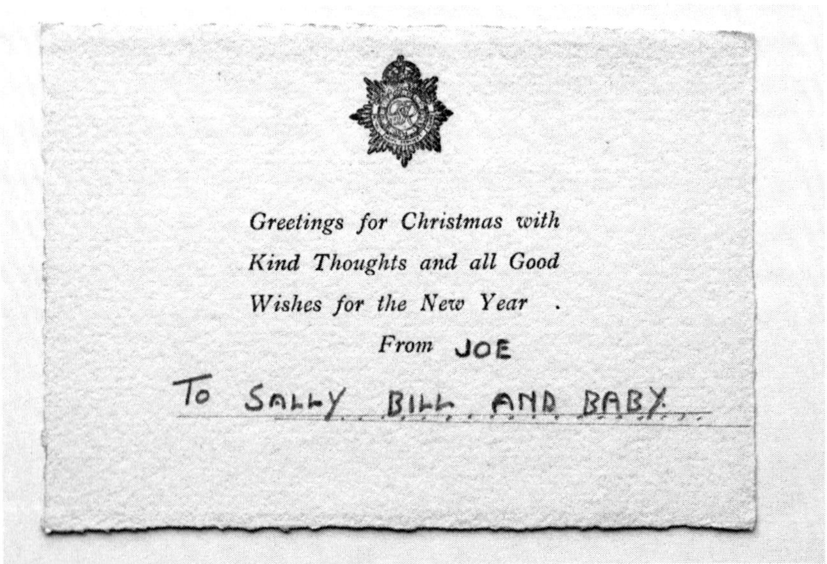

1944 Christmas Card

We also have three more photographs taken in 1945, where Joe and his regiment had by then been sent to Hong Kong via India.

The first has Joe, standing tall in a swimsuit, and written on the back is: Juhu Beach, India, 1945. The second is of Joe and a friend with two Indian snake-charmers, complete with basket and pipes. Written on the back of this one is: Bombay, India, 5/11/45. To James and Lucy, from Joe.

The third one has Joe sitting on the bonnet of his truck and written on the back is: 25/12/45 Christmas Day! To Mother, from Joe. This photograph is the one placed at the beginning of this chapter and, maybe, the only one of Joe taken in Hong Kong! So few photographs were taken at this time of war, and how precious these few are!

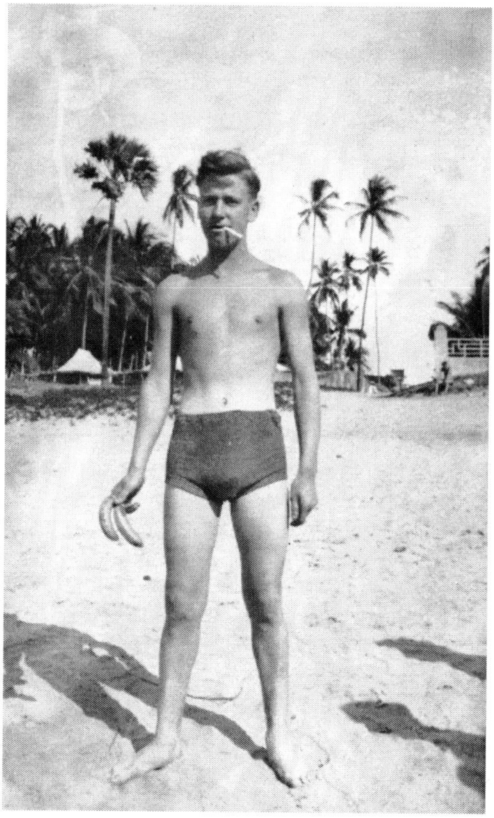

Joe on Juhu Beach, India, 1945

Joe seated, with snake charmers, Bombay, India 1945

Defeated, Germany had surrendered on May 8th, 1945 and after America dropped two Atomic bombs on Japan in August 1945, they too surrendered.

Great relief was felt by all nations that the war, which had touched the whole world was over, but now there was the mammoth task of repatriating prisoners of war, of clearing up bombed areas and also of helping the war-torn countries to rebuild.

Joe's parents, John and Sarah Hughes, were now not quite so worried about their son so far away from home, and, in 1946, their son, James, was now safely home from his world travels with the Royal Navy. Still living at home, was the boy's young brother, Frank, who had been exempted from national service by being in a reserved occupation.

Like so many other soldiers, Joe, with his regiment, 387 Company, RASC, had been redeployed to Hong Kong. Sent to deal with the aftermath of the years of fighting in this far region. Stopping off in India, on the way, as our photographs show. Then, at the end of 1945, they found themselves stationed on the coast in the Wan Chai District of the little island of Hong Kong, which is situated off the mainland Hong Kong District of Kowloon in the South China seas.

It had been part of Colonial Britain since 1841, but in December 1941, the Japanese Imperial Army entered and captured the British bunker on the strategic Wong Nai Chung Gap, and thereafter occupied Hong Kong until the British liberation in 1945.

Writing from Hong Kong, Joe said that their first billet had been at Happy Valley Racecourse, which gave them a great view to watch the horse racing there on Sundays. His soldier mate, Ian Cameron, has said that, when off duty, they often used to catch the Star Ferry from the Island across to Kowloon, to visit the busy market area, where all the little fishing boats came in. They enjoyed being welcomed by the local people, who were so happy to see the British Army back again, after the great wartime ordeal of occupation the island had been through.

On March 16th 1946, Joseph wrote a letter in response to one from his brother, James. It had been addressed to Mrs James Hughes (Lucy) of 56, Cavendish Street, Glasgow C5. It had been sent by Field Post on March 19th. On the envelope, Joseph had written: 'On Active Service', together with his name and number.

In what was to be his very last letter home, Joseph began by remarking that he had recently received three letters all at once, from James, from his mother and, even, from his brother, Frank, which had amused him no end.

"I nearly died, when I knew it was from him, as, at first I thought it was from the old man, until it asked me for a bladder, then I knew it would not be him, for I don't think he plays football. And Frank said he was up the Queens Park with you and Chris, having some snaps taken, and he is going to send me one, if they come out OK.

I think you will know by now, I have got my teeth out and, when I get them in, I shall try and get a half decent photograph taken, I shall send one to you and mother- that's if they come out OK."

He then commented on James's recent demobilisation: *"Well by your letter you seem to be dead pleased with your demob suit, if only I could get one of them. It shall be a good while before I get it. I am only grade sixty-three that's all, let's pray for grade sixty-three and over.*

I hope by the time you get this letter you have got a job and settled down again into that horrible thing called 'Civvy Street'. I bet you are a lot happier.

Well, there is another horse race in our camp next Sunday, and we have got the best places for watching it from our billets. I don't know if I told you, we are stationed in the racecourse and they are smashing billets.

Well, tell Lucy I was asking for her and the Family"

He signed off with the words, 'From your brother, Joe, to ex-AB J Hughes', and a heart-felt PS 'WRITE SOON'. This is a lovely special letter from brother to brother, we can see how close they were as a family and the warmth of the sentiments are moving to read. A young man of nineteen, so far away from friends and family, his thoughts lay always back home in 'Bonnie Scotland'.

Sadly, this was his last known letter, kept safe and sound by his sister, Sally, and, the last words of contact he had with his family, as, five days later, on March 21st, he was to make the ultimate sacrifice, and to die two days later on March 23rd, doing his duty for his country in Hong Kong.

One of the missions of the RASC was to clear the arsenal of bombs and ammunition left by the retreating Japanese Army, carefully moving it from built-up civilian areas by truck to a safer place.

March 21st was just a usual working morning for Joe and his pals. They had loaded their trucks with the live Japanese ammunition. Joe with his lorry was leading the convoy, when the terrible tragedy occurred.

As to what happened next, I have combined some family memories with details from the army's official report. This had been written later, in 1984, by an Army Unit Correspondent, who was attending a memorial dedication service held in 1984 at The Lyemun Barracks, Hong Kong, to honour the actions of Joseph Hughes GC.

'The gallantry dates back to March 1946. When the forces returned to the colony in late 1945, they found that, among many horrors, the Japanese had left considerable quantities of loose, potentially dangerous explosives. These munitions had been stored precariously in the ARP shelters in Happy Valley.

It was decided that the materials should be transferred from Happy Valley to Lyemun depot as a temporary storage before final disposal. A convoy of military vehicles from RASC in Hong Kong was detailed to carry out the movement, and Joseph Hughes was the driver of the leading vehicle.

As the convoy was proceeding to the ammunition depot via North Point past Taikoo Dock Yard, through Shau Ki Wan, then up the hill to Lyemun Barracks, the second vehicle saw signs of fire coming from Joseph Hughes's lorry.

All efforts to attract him were in vain, and he continued his journey to the Barracks camp, and then, down the hill to the magazine. He reversed up the entrance to the magazine and stopped.

As he dismounted from the cab, it was only then he saw that his vehicle had caught fire, possibly by sparks from his engine. Shouting for his working comrades and local people living nearby to leave the area, he hurriedly picked up a fire extinguisher and went to put out the fire on the burning camouflage net on his truck, desperately disregarding the danger he was encountering from the magazine beside his now adjacent lorry.

He also knew full well that, besides normal holdings for the Lyemun coast battery, there were quantities of six-inch B.L.S.A.P.B.C. Shell, 4.5in Howitzer cartridges, captured Japanese ammunition and a quantity of Happy Valley explosive materials stored there. Realising the consequences to the surrounding area if it blew up, he fought the fire until all his clothing was burning, then tried to get his truck away from the danger of explosions to all locals living nearby. Accordingly, instead of casualties, which might have been heavy, only Driver Hughes ultimately lost his life.

Meanwhile, the through-draught into the entrance sucked the fire into the magazine, causing combustion, so that Joe's truck and the nearby lorry both blew up, with a cataclysmic explosion, causing a landslide and the disappearance of a large part of the hillside.

Afterwards, his comrades found Joseph lying wounded on the hillside. Still alive, he was then taken to hospital, but died two days later from the severe burns he had received, trying to put out the devastating fire.

Driver Hughes's courage in remaining at his task, thereby attempting to minimise the danger to others, when he could have run for safety, was an outstanding example of devotion to duty.'

Joseph's wrecked truck, March 21st 1946

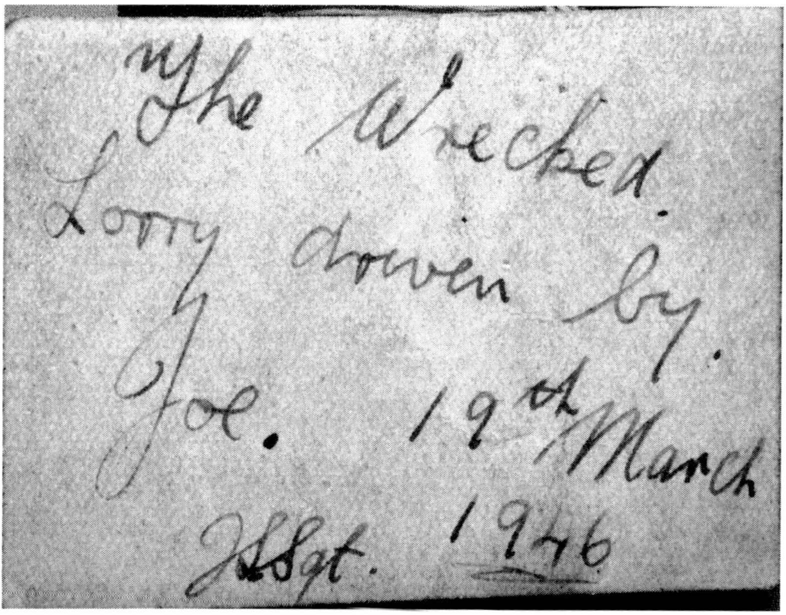

The back of the photograph of Joseph's truck

Joseph's Funeral, the Army and the Hughes Family

What a terrible shock for his family back home in Glasgow, all so unexpected, as the war was now over. They were so helpless in their grief, not even able to attend his funeral, so many thousands of miles away, on the other side of the world.

His comrades also grieved to lose a friend, as Joe had been a very popular, happy young man, only 19 years 6 months old and always so full of singing and fun. It was said that, afterwards, whenever passing the spot where Joe was fatally wounded, all his comrades stopped to pay tribute and to salute their brave friend.

During the Japanese occupation, many local people had lost their homes. There had also been a big influx of refugees from surrounding areas affected by the turmoil of war, so they had all set up temporary villages of huts and tented homes on the hillsides by the beaches. Joseph had shouted to these nearby people, warning them of the danger and urging them to leave the area, as he knew the danger presented by his burning truck.

As a thank you for the brave deed he had done, trying to help all, they later requested that Joseph be buried in their own Happy Valley civil cemetery, which the Army agreed to. His body was first taken to lie in St Joseph's RC Church, Wan Chi, until his burial.

On the day of the ceremony, conducted with full military honours, a sequence of photographs was taken to send home to his grieving mother, father and family. These have been carefully kept over the years, latterly being found in 1995 at our late parents' home, the home of Joe's sister, Sally, and brother-in law, Bill Goad.

These are reproduced in sequence next.

Joseph Hughes Military Funeral

Hong Kong - March 1946

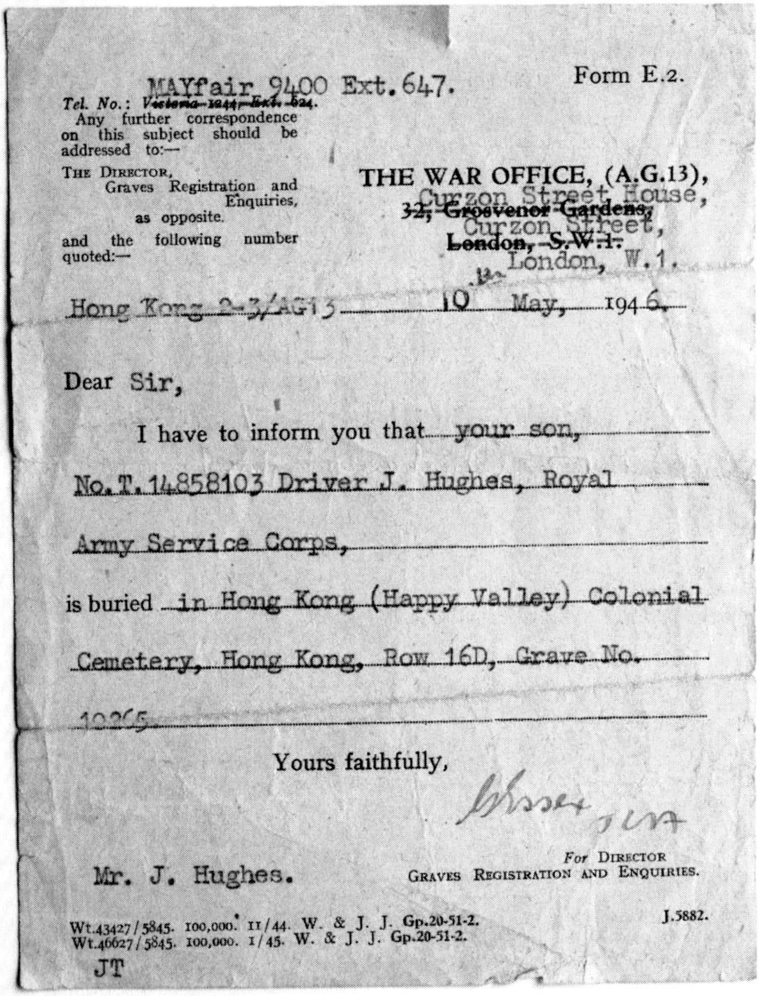

MAYfair 9400 Ext. 647.

Form E.2.

Tel. No.: ~~Victoria 1244, Ext. 624.~~

Any further correspondence on this subject should be addressed to:—

THE DIRECTOR,
Graves Registration and Enquiries,
as opposite.

and the following number quoted:—

Hong Kong 2-3/AG13

THE WAR OFFICE, (A.G.13),
Curzon Street House,
~~32, Grosvenor Gardens,~~
Curzon Street,
~~London, S.W.1.~~
London, W.1.

10th May, 1946.

Dear Sir,

I have to inform you that your son, No. T.14858103 Driver J. Hughes, Royal Army Service Corps,

is buried in Hong Kong (Happy Valley) Colonial Cemetery, Hong Kong, Row 16D, Grave No. 10265.

Yours faithfully,

For DIRECTOR
GRAVES REGISTRATION AND ENQUIRIES.

Mr. J. Hughes.

Wt.43427/5845. 100,000. 11/44. W. & J. J. Gp.20-51-2.
Wt.46627/5845. 100,000. 1/45. W. & J. J. Gp.20-51-2.

J.5882.

JT

Original Note from the War Office

The family were then to receive a number of communications from the Army. Early on, Joe's Commanding Officer, Major Grimshaw, had sent the family a letter of condolence, to which John Hughes had replied.

Then on 6th May, Joe's father received a reply from Major Grimshaw to his letter, thanking John for his letter and for the appreciation he had expressed. He reiterated the details of Joseph's heroic act, pointing out that he had courageously attempted to put out the fire, when he could easily have run away and escaped.

He then said: "For this courageous act, I have recommended him for a medal." Finally, Major Grimshaw informed John Hughes that the men of the Company were 'putting up a very excellent monument at his grave'. So, the regiment was determined to celebrate Joseph's heroism and, already, the award of a medal was being mooted!

Next, on 10th May 1946, Joe's father and mother received a letter from the War Office to inform them that their son was buried in Hong Kong (Happy Valley) Colonial Cemetery. It was just a small, typed, bureaucratic note, seen here.

There was also an official notification from the War Graves Commission, how far away they must have felt and how distant it must all have seemed to them! At the same time, how proud they must have been of their son!

One Year Later: A Headstone and a George Cross

On the first anniversary of Joseph's death in March 1947, his Commanding Officer, Major Grimshaw, of the RASC, sent John and Sarah Hughes a further letter of condolence and, with it, a photograph of Joseph's grave, now with its magnificent granite and marble headstone monument, inlaid with the regimental badge above his inscription.

What a wonderful tribute to have erected and paid for by his comrades of the Royal Army Service Corps. Also, his comrades laid a wonderful floral wreath there in his memory, in the form of the regimental badge.

The inscription reads:

IN MEMORY OF

T/14858103

DRIVER JOSEPH HUGHES

387 COY RASC GT

DIED ON DUTY 23rd MARCH 1946

AGED 20 YEARS

RIP

ERECTED BY THE OFFICERS, NCOs & MEN

OF HIS COMPANY

Photograph received from Major Grimshaw, one year on

Also, arriving from Hong Kong in 1947, were the following photographs, taken by Lady Nedderburn, the wife of Lord Nedderburn, Minister of Foreign Affairs, Peking, China.

Joseph's grave

View of Hong Kong taken from back of grave, 1947

On 21st May 1947, John Hughes wrote a letter to show the family's appreciation of Joe's comrades' thoughtfulness, in which he expressed the following sentiments:

'On behalf of my wife and myself, I wish to express my sincere thanks for the beautiful memorial you and your Company have placed on my son Joseph's grave. It is a very great tribute you have paid to his memory. Neither I nor my wife could have wished for anything better. The fact that you remembered my boy on the first anniversary of his death is also something I very much appreciate, and, as it was impossible for me to pay a personal visit, the fact that he was not forgotten is a source of great comfort to us at home. Thank you also for sending the photograph and so enabling us to fully appreciate the great tribute you have paid to my dear son.

We still feel his death very deeply, but somehow the knowledge that some of our grief seems to be shared by you very human people, helps us to carry on.

There is not much more I can say, so I hope and trust that you will accept our sincerest thanks and realise that what you have done, helped to ease our pain and will be appreciated as long as we live.

Very best wishes to all of the Company and the hope for a speedy and safe return.'

From this well constructed and beautifully worded letter, we can clearly see that, even after over a year, thoughts of Joe were forever in his family's minds and, not long afterwards, a letter arrived at 159, Pollockshaws Road, addressed to John Hughes. Sent from Ore Place, Hastings, Sussex, England, it was from Joseph's regimental records officer, dated 8th July 1947 and it stated the following:

'Dear Sir,

I am proud to inform you that your son the late T/14858103 Driver Joseph Hughes, has been awarded the George Cross for his conspicuous gallantry in Hong Kong on 21st March, 1946. I am enclosing an extract from the supplement to the London Gazette *of Tuesday the 24th June, 1947, notifying the award.'*

The Colonel then finishes with the ultimate accolade, noting that this was "*the first award of the George Cross to a serving member of the Royal Army Service Corps, and it is my sincere hope that this recognition of your son's bravery may help you in your grief.*"

The Citation read:

The George Cross

(Posthumous)

T/14858103 Driver Joseph Hughes

Royal Army Service Corps

On 21st March 1946, at Lyemun Barracks, Hong Kong, Driver Hughes was driving a three-ton vehicle carrying ammunition and explosives into the magazine at Lyemun Barracks. As his vehicle was entering the magazine area, it started to smoulder and then it caught fire. Knowing full well that his vehicle was likely to blow up at any moment, Driver Hughes, instead of running for safety, did everything in his power to put out the fire. Notwithstanding small explosions occurring in his vehicle, he first tried to remove the burning camouflage net. He then tried fire extinguishers which failed. A few minutes later, his lorry blew up, fatally injuring him. By his action, the explosion was delayed and warning was given to troops in the locality, who were able to take cover. Accordingly, casualties which might have been heavy, were negligible, except for Driver Hughes's fatal injury.

Driver Hughes's courage in remaining at his task, thereby attempting to minimise the danger to others, when he could have run to safety, was an outstanding devotion to duty.

London Gazette, *26th June, 1947.*

The George Cross

In 1940, King George VI was so moved by acts of courage during the Blitz, particularly in bomb and mine disposal, that on 24th September of that year, he instituted the order of The George Cross for 'acts of the greatest heroism or of the most conspicuous courage in circumstances of extreme danger,' when not in the face of the enemy.

The George Cross Ranks equally with the Victoria Cross as a 'Tier 1' award for bravery and, if both are won, it is worn immediately after it. The George Cross has been awarded both to civilians and to military personnel, sometimes posthumously.

Made of silver, on one side is depicted St. George slaying the dragon, with the inscription, 'For Gallantry', and on the other side appears the name of the holder and the date of the award. The cross is suspended from a dark blue ribbon threaded through a silver bar adorned with laurel leaves.

Joseph's father and mother were so proud that his king and country had honoured their son in this way.

Glasgow press tribute, 1947

Not surprisingly, Glasgow's own newspaper, *The Daily Record*, was quick to pick up on this story of the award of a George Cross to a local Glaswegian lad. There was a big headline on the front page – "GC Scot Died To Save Others", with a report of the heroic incident and a photograph of Joseph sitting on the bonnet of his truck.

More courage in the extended Hughes family

This was a doubly interesting local story, as, not five years earlier, John Hughes's son-in-law, Bill Goad – Joseph's brother-in-law – had been awarded the Albert Medal, which was the naval equivalent of the George Cross. He had been a nineteen-year-old Leading Seaman on HMS *Ashanti*, a destroyer on Russian convoy duty. He had volunteered to go overboard into freezing waters, to help save drowning crew members of the *Somali*, which had been massively damaged by a U-boat in September 1942.

The destroyer was being towed by the *Ashanti*, which had only a skeleton crew still on board ship, when it was broken in two in very rough Arctic seas. Only 35 of the remaining 102 crew had been saved. Unknown to Bill at the time, by his individual action, he later discovered, he had saved the life of the *Somali's* captain.

Bill Goad had married his wife, Sally Hughes, just before they had gone down to the Palace to collect his own decoration in July 1943.

Added Marble Tribute, 1947

At this time, Joseph's regiment paid two further tributes to their hero. First, they placed a marble plaque on his grave in Happy Valley, detailing his award of the George Cross. The words inscribed on it were:

DRIVER JOSEPH HUGHES WAS

POSTHUMOUSLY AWARDED THE GEORGE CROSS

FOR OUTSTANDING DEVOTION TO DUTY

Secondly, another marble memorial stone was laid in the grounds of Lyemun Barracks, close to where Joseph lost his life. This would be a place to remind all recruits of the need for devotion to duty; an annual remembrance service would also be held there.

Understandably, Joe's father and mother were really proud that their son had been signally honoured by his king and country. John Hughes, especially, having been a serving soldier in WWI, fully comprehended the significance and scope of Joe's heroic act.

Lyemun Barracks Memorial, 2016
Kenny Yu of the Hong Kong Royal British Legion and Simon So, of the Hong Kong Ex-servicemen's' Association

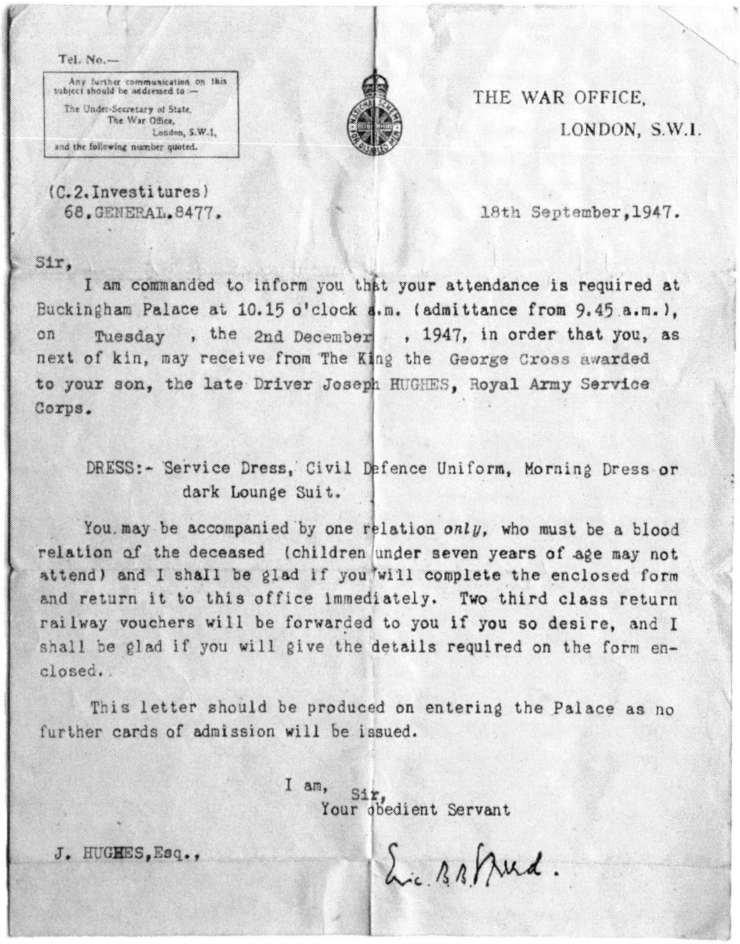

Tel. No.—

Any further communication on this subject should be addressed to:—
The Under-Secretary of State,
The War Office,
London, S.W.1,
and the following number quoted.

THE WAR OFFICE,
LONDON, S.W.1.

(C.2.Investitures)
68.GENERAL.8477.

18th September,1947.

Sir,

I am commanded to inform you that your attendance is required at Buckingham Palace at 10.15 o'clock a.m. (admittance from 9.45 a.m.), on Tuesday , the 2nd December , 1947, in order that you, as next of kin, may receive from The King the George Cross awarded to your son, the late Driver Joseph HUGHES, Royal Army Service Corps.

DRESS:- Service Dress, Civil Defence Uniform, Morning Dress or dark Lounge Suit.

You may be accompanied by one relation *only*, who must be a blood relation of the deceased (children under seven years of age may not attend) and I shall be glad if you will complete the enclosed form and return it to this office immediately. Two third class return railway vouchers will be forwarded to you if you so desire, and I shall be glad if you will give the details required on the form enclosed.

This letter should be produced on entering the Palace as no further cards of admission will be issued.

I am, Sir,
Your obedient Servant

J. HUGHES,Esq.,

Eric B.B. Bird.

The letter from the War Office:
Invitation to go to Buckingham Palace

Not only that, for, as we saw, not five years earlier, John's son-in-law, Bill Goad, had been honoured by the King at Buckingham Palace for the heroic act he had performed at sea. The difference was, of course, that Bill had survived, unlike John's son, Joe.

In addition, his earlier letter to Joe's Commanding Officer had been immaculately expressed, as we saw. What came over were John's quiet, natural dignity and his simple gratitude to Major Grimshaw, for the way in which he had handled the whole matter. These same characteristics came through again in the letter John sent to him on 25th November, reproduced here in its entirety:

Dear Major Grimshaw,

I am sorry for not writing sooner, as I was waiting for the official word from the War Office about my son's award of the George Cross.

I have been informed to be at Buckingham Palace on Tuesday 2nd December 1947 at 10.15 am to receive the George Cross from the King.

Myself and Mrs Hughes will be at the Palace on that date.

You will be pleased to know that I had some of your boys from your COY 983 RASC up seeing myself and Mrs Hughes. If ever you and your wife are up in Scotland, I would be pleased to have a visit from you and your wife. I hope that yourself and Mrs Grimshaw are enjoying Civvy life and settled down now after being away overseas so long.

I haven't much more to say, only that I will feel a proud man on Tuesday morning, when I receive the George Cross from the King.

Sincerely John Hughes

John and Sarah Hughes made the long journey from Glasgow to London on the morning of the 2nd December, Sarah in her best dress, coat and hat, John wearing a suit borrowed from his son James. They were obviously striving to look their best in those austere times of rationing and clothes coupons in the post war era of the 1940s.

It was a bitter sweet day full of emotions for them but one of great pride in the memory of their son Joseph and of receiving The George Cross at Buckingham Palace, personally presented to them by King George VI and Queen Elizabeth on behalf of a grateful country.

The Hughes family were right to sense something special about Joseph's Commanding Officer, for, in Major Bob Grimshaw's 2002 obituary, it stated that Bob was punctilious in ensuring that this act of extreme bravery be recognised with the highest award available, the George Cross, one of only three achieved by the RASC.

Joseph's father and mother certainly felt that the regiment had dealt with the whole situation with great compassion to them as a family, especially after their sympathetic personal contact with Major Grimshaw.

The years passed by for the family, but no-one ever forgot Joseph. In 1949, their son, James, emigrated to Australia, and by 1955, their daughter, Sally, had three sons. John and Sarah used to travel down to Stretham for their annual holidays, while Bill and Sally Goad often went up to Glasgow.

In 1958, Sarah Hughes had a street accident. She was out shopping one Saturday morning, when she was knocked down by a lorry on the corner of Kingston and Bridge Street and was taken to the Glasgow Royal Infirmary. After having had stitches in her cut arm and a badly bruised leg bound up, she then discharged herself and took the bus home.

Husband, John, and son, Frank, later found her dazed and wandering in Cumberland Street, and Sarah was unable to remember anything of her previous accident. Later, the local police said there was nothing they could do, as the lorry drove on, and no witnesses to the event had come forward.

The sad fact was that Sarah had become acutely deaf at this time and she never really recovered from the shock. The shock of the accident added to her other growing health problems. Her health was failing, and John had heart trouble, too, so, the consequences of all this were that, by 1964, both had sadly passed away.

Sarah and grandsons at River Meadows, Stretham

John and Sarah Hughes at River Meadows, Stretham.

With grandsons Patrick, Martin and Christopher

George Cross Sale, 1965

So, at this time, the family made the decision to sell Joseph's George Cross, thinking it was the best and safest option for all. This was the first George Cross ever to be auctioned, and the sale took place in Christie's London salerooms, on March 16th 1965.

The family were very happy, when they heard Joseph's medal had been bought on behalf of the Royal Army Service Corps Club, based at Joseph's Regimental home, which, at that time, was in Buller Barracks, Aldershot. A fitting place for the medal to go.

This special logistic regiment has a rich heritage, dating back to the 13th century, having once been known as 'The Waggoners', owing to their long history of moving equipment with horse and waggon. This had also been the name of their regimental magazine at this time. Since 1993, the regiment has been known as The Royal Logistic Corps and its base moved to Deepcut Barracks, Surrey.

Their motto is 'We Sustain', so its present magazine is now aptly called 'The Sustainer'. The Royal Logistic Corps museum is at Deepcut Barracks, and also in the nearby Officers' Mess, there is Joseph's George Cross, proudly displayed in a case with other regimental regalia. This can be viewed there by appointment.

Royal Logistics Corps Officers' Mess, Deepcut, Surrey.

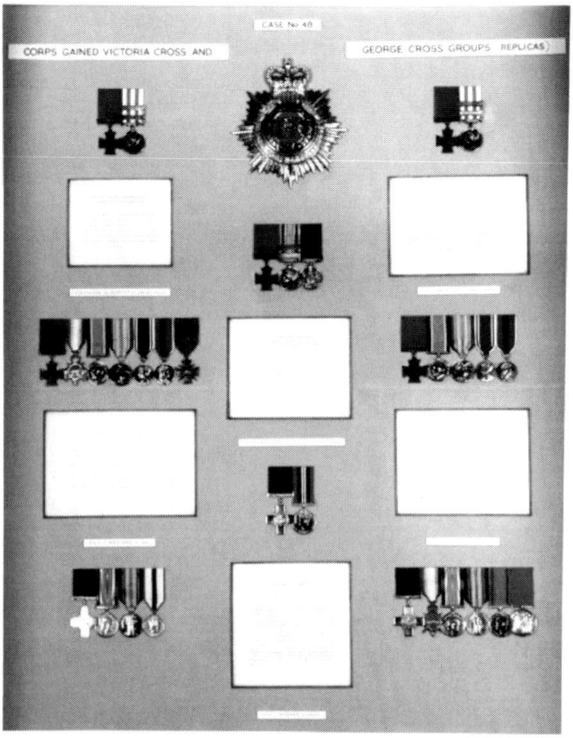

Joseph Hughes's GC Medal in the centre of case

Today, beside his medals in their case, there is a framed drawing of Joseph Hughes GC by artist Jane Adams, specially commissioned by the Royal Logistics Corps.

Photograph of the drawing

The Hornet, front cover
(Image reproduced courtesy of D C Thompson & Co Ltd.)

Joseph's heroism finds a wider audience

In addition to these new tributes paid to Joseph by his regiment, in 1970, much to Joseph's family's pleasure, he was pictured in full colour on the front cover of *The Hornet*. This boys' comic was one of several produced by the Dundee publishers, D C Thompson, who also produced *The Wizard, The Rover* and *The Hotspur*, among many others. The comics were full of patriotic tales, of war heroes and, specifically, of ordinary young men and boys, who had been involved in great adventures.

They were read a lot by boys from the 1920s onwards and were still flourishing in the 1960s and 1970s. We can easily imagine how proud the Hughes family would have been to see a picture of their son emblazoned on the front cover and his name and his story appearing on page 15, under the heading 'The *Hornet* Gallery of Courage'.

In 2016, the Hughes family purchased a copy of this comic and had it framed. Irene Hughes-Finn, Joseph's cousin, subsequently presented the framed comic to The Lord Provost at Joseph's 70th Memorial service, held at the St. Francis Centre. This now hangs proudly in Glasgow City Hall.

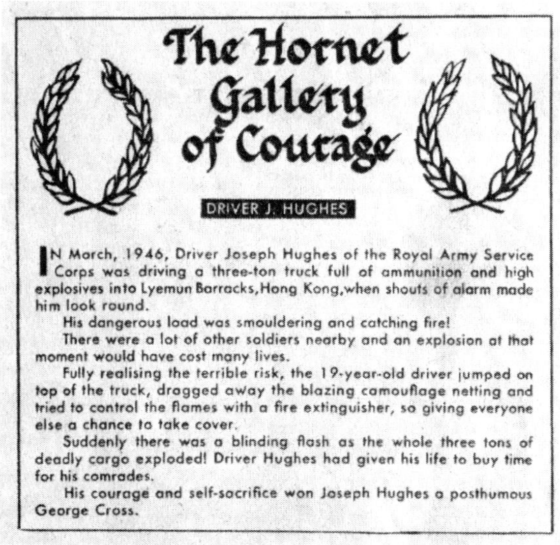

The Hornet Gallery of Courage

DRIVER J. HUGHES

IN March, 1946, Driver Joseph Hughes of the Royal Army Service Corps was driving a three-ton truck full of ammunition and high explosives into Lyemun Barracks, Hong Kong, when shouts of alarm made him look round.

His dangerous load was smouldering and catching fire!

There were a lot of other soldiers nearby and an explosion at that moment would have cost many lives.

Fully realising the terrible risk, the 19-year-old driver jumped on top of the truck, dragged away the blazing camouflage netting and tried to control the flames with a fire extinguisher, so giving everyone else a chance to take cover.

Suddenly there was a blinding flash as the whole three tons of deadly cargo exploded! Driver Hughes had given his life to buy time for his comrades.

His courage and self-sacrifice won Joseph Hughes a posthumous George Cross.

The Hornet, inside report
(Image reproduced courtesy of D C Thompson & Co Ltd.)

Regimental Tribute in Hong Kong, 1976

In 1976, The Transport Office, Royal Army Service Corps invited their former Commanding Officer, Major Bob Grimshaw, to go out to Hong Kong to lay a wreath on Joseph's grave at Happy Valley to represent the Regiment at a special 30-year anniversary service of remembrance.

Major Bob Grimshaw, laying tribute wreath, 1976

During WWII, in 1943, 387 Company RASC changed its role and became a DUKW Amphibious Company, but, when sent on deployment to Hong Kong, it became a General Transport (GT) Company again. However, in 1946, Joseph, in his last letter, gave his address as, RASC, Amphibians, c/o APO Hong Kong. When questioned recently at Deepcut Barracks about this, Lt Col Knowles said he felt it showed they were still proud to be called Amphibians.

As we saw, *The Waggoner* was the Journal of the Royal Army Service Corps and, we were delighted to identify the following extracts concerning further ways of honouring Driver Joseph Hughes.

In December 1980, Hong Kong RASC received a new replacement boat, a brand-new range of safety craft, named 'Joseph Hughes GC' and a small plaque has been placed in the wheelhouse, engraved with the story of his heroic deed.

It is a Talisman class vessel, which has added a new dimension to the RCT fleet out there, and, at last, a craft that can beat the ten-knot barrier – and do it twice over!

Now they are managing to keep pace with the demands of the garrison and the Hong Kong Government to move almost anything anywhere.

In December 1981, Hong Kong 29th Squadron are on the move to a new home and have decided to call their new complex 'The Hughes Building', as a tribute to DVR Hughes GC, who tragically lost his life at Lyemun Barracks in 1946.

In November 1984, the Army General Service launch, 'Joseph Hughes GC', made her last trip in Hong Kong waters, prior to returning home. Like her famous namesake, she too has served the Colony well!

All show the continuing pride the RASC had in their first George Cross hero.

Memorial stone moved into Gurkha care, Hong Kong, 1984

In 1984, Joseph's memorial stone was taken from its original 1946 site – the scene of his selfless act at the ammunition depot – to be re-erected at Gun Club Barracks in the care of the Gurkha Transport Regiment, as the garrison was soon to be handed over to the Hong Kong Government.

A dedication parade and service took place there on November 11th 1984, attended by the Commanding Officer and all the unit representatives. The padre was accompanied by an RCT driver, carrying a huge cross, which was placed by a lone peepal tree near the re-erected memorial stone. This tree is traditionally holy to the Gurkha and is always planted with religious significance. The Gurkhas even presented one to be planted at Buller Barracks, Camberley, in the event of Joseph's memorial being returned to England, when the regiment left Hong Kong.

The following is as described by a Unit Correspondent:

The chaplain opened his small bible and, standing at the head of the stone, solemnly pronounced the following words: 'This stone commemorates the bravery of Joseph Hughes, Driver of the Royal Army Service Corps, for which he was awarded the George Cross, posthumously. The stone has been moved on the departure of British Troops from the scene of his selfless act at Lyemun Barracks, Hong Kong Island, and brought here into the care of the Gurkha Transport Regiment and the Royal Corps of Transport.'

He ended with the words, 'Lest we Forget.'

And, indeed, through the years, the Royal Army Service Corps have always continued to honour their comrade each year on Remembrance Day. However, there have been many years of change in Hong Kong, and it is now no longer a Colonial outpost of Great Britain, having been handed back to the Government of China in 1997. But Joseph's memorial was to stay in Hong Kong.

Joseph Hughes GC, First Day Cover, 1990

Next, Joseph Hughes's country gave him a particularly interesting accolade. In 1990, it was the 50th anniversary of the institution of the George Cross by King George VI and the Government of Great Britain in September 1940. Joseph Hughes GC and his story were commemorated in a First Day Cover series with a special George Cross stamp commemorating these 50 years of gallantry.

This First Day Cover was one of twenty-one different ones, issued on 11th September 1990, and celebrating a number of different medals, as well as the armed forces of World War II.

We have recently acquired what purports to be the last available copy of this First Day Cover.

First Day Cover Stamps

A further matter of note is that, on the Cover itself, located beside the stamps, there is what appears to be a painting of Joseph's act of heroism in Hong Kong. This may have given Irene – as is described in the next chapter – the idea of having a similar one painted by a local Glaswegian artist.

Memorial stone returned to Lyemun Barracks, Hong Kong, 1996

Throughout these times of political change, Joseph's memorial stone has been taken care of by his regiment. Fifty years later, in 1996, it was finally moved to its present resting place back at Lyemun Barracks, on a bank beside the old regimental Chapel, not far from where the heroic incident took place.

A service is held there, and a wreath of red poppies is still laid by a representative of the Hong Kong Royal British Legion and the Hong Kong Ex-servicemen's Association, each year on 11th November, the National Remembrance Day.

This former Barracks is now the Lei Yue Mun Holiday Camp, maintained by the Hong Kong Urban Council.

Fifty Years On, Glasgow Sunday Mail, 1996

A report in the *Glasgow Sunday Mail*, March 10th 1996, had the following headline: 'Hong Kong tribute to Joe', and there was a photograph of Joe sitting on his truck. In the article, it said: 'Brave solider, Joseph Hughes, is Scotland's forgotten hero'.

It told the story of fifty years before, of his heroism, and of the future tribute that would be held in honour of his memory on March 21st 1996, by the Royal Army Service Corps commanders and soldiers at Lyemun Barracks in Hong Kong. It also said that, on that same day in Glasgow, his cousin, Irene Finn would attend a small service in her local Catholic Church. I shall deal with this event again in the chapter 'Irene's story'.

Glasgow memorial sixty years on, 2006

A memorial plaque was unveiled to Joseph Hughes GC in the Gorbals St. Francis Centre, Glasgow, March 2006. It consisted of a glass-fronted box, with, in its centre, a facsimile of Joseph's George Cross, and his campaign medal with photographs and tributes to him. This was the culmination of Cousin Irene's years of campaigning, to be described later.

Also at this time, a representative of the Royal Logistic Corps Association laid a wreath on Driver Hughes's grave in Happy Valley Cemetery, Hong Kong.

An article in the regimental magazine, sixty years on, reported the award of the George Cross to Captain Peter Norton GC. The Royal Army Logistic Corps was very proud of this, their second GC, reminding us just how rare a bravery award of this kind had been for the regiment.

Joseph's Full Story Seventy Years On, 2016

Joseph Hughes's young life was cut short at 19 years of age, but he really made his mark in the immediate post-war world, and the story of his heroism was to live on in so many ways. Of his brave actions in Hong Kong on March 21st 1946, and of his country's recognition, with the award to him of the George Cross, we have already had a big story to tell the world.

Then, we have had the story of the way his regiment took pride in their fallen hero and the way that his name has lived on out in Hong Kong. And how they bought, and now display, his medals in the regimental museum back home.

Next, there has been the whole story of his memorial stone in Hong Kong at the old Lyemun Barracks, and his grave placed in Happy Valley by the grateful local people, and the headstone paid for by his comrades.

After describing the whole sequence of events, which took place during the half-century following Joseph's death, we have almost come to the point where the story of developments in the 21st century can be fully told. This concerns the way in which, eventually, Joseph was to be fully honoured in his home city of Glasgow.

Clearly, this story of Joseph Hughes's heroism is destined, in the first place, for other members of the Hughes family and their descendants, so that they might now be able to take pride in him, and in the wider recognition he still has in Britain and in Hong Kong to this day. But, we are also really happy to be able to share our story with others, who may take an interest in a family story of this kind.

Finally, on a personal note, these written memories are being passed on in the belief that they might inspire future generations. We trust that this story of Joseph's character and courage will have assured the brave young man of some kind of immortality and guarantee that he will never be forgotten.

Badge of the Royal Army Service Corps

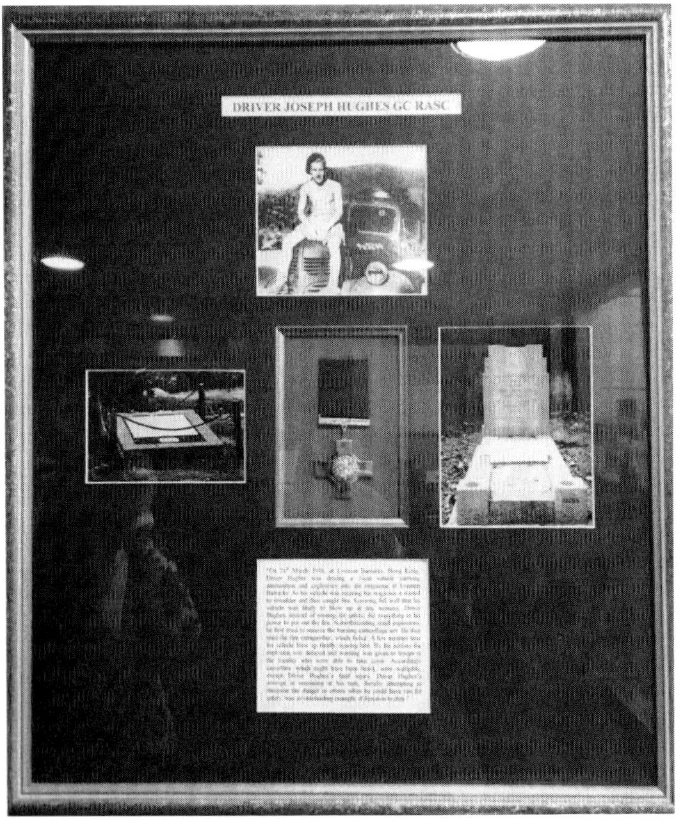

St. Francis memorial plaque

Joseph's Memorial Tribute, 2006

In 2002, at the Gorbals Fair, at the St. Francis Centre, Glasgow, Irene Hughes-Finn had been presented with a new plaque commemorating Joseph Hughes GC – bringing a fruitful conclusion to the years of campaigning by his cousin.

On the 60th anniversary of Joseph's heroic act, in 2006, an official public unveiling ceremony gave the plaque a permanent home here.

We have, at last, made the encounter of another extraordinary member of this Glasgow Hughes family, Irene, whose story is closely intertwined with that of her older cousin, Joseph.

Putting You in the Picture. Meeting Irene

In July 2015, after a month's correspondence with our newly found Hughes cousin, Irene, I was sent a package of papers, letters and photographs, representing her long years of effort to bring the memory of her cousin, Joseph Hughes GC, to the present-day people of the City of Glasgow. I was completely taken aback by her tenacity, which had eventually been rewarded with a Memorial Tribute in the Gorbals St. Francis Community Centre in 2006.

She also wrote me a letter asking, if I would fulfil her dream and be her 'Book Angel' and write Joseph's story for all to know. After great thought, and aware of the research and work which would be entailed, three months later, I wrote to her, accepting her challenge!

The idea had come into my mind of combining Joseph's and James's lives, intertwining them with her and with myself, in a much wider family story, in which Fate appeared to be bringing us all together at that time.

For these reasons, this next chapter is Irene's story. Without her valiant efforts, and the earnest request she made in her letter to me, this book might never have been written at all. And all these family stories never told.

Chapter Three

Irene's Story – 'A Devoted Cousin'

Catherine (Irene) Hughes - Finn

1937-2016

Irene at 60th anniversary tribute at St. Francis Centre, 2006

Baby Irene and her cousin, Sally Hughes-Goad

Catherine 'Irene' Hughes-Finn – A Devoted Cousin

Irene Hughes was born 2nd January 1937, the first child of Charles and Esther Hughes. Although christened Catherine, in honour of her paternal Grandmother, she was always known as Irene by her family. She was later joined by two younger brothers, Charlie and Kenny.

She attended St. Francis Primary School and then went on to Garnethill Convent on Hill Street, Glasgow, near the Art School In the city centre. As a child, she had happy memories of playing in the back streets of the Gorbals, where her many Hughes cousins lived. Her cousin, Sally, is seen holding her in the nearby photograph, but she was especially fond of Sally's brother, her cousin, Joseph. She loved his visits to her home and playing with his little dog, Trixie. Joe was always full of fun, singing and laughter, and she called him by her special name of 'Josie'.

Although only eight years old, she always remembered the day in 1945, when he came to pay his last visit to his uncle and aunt to say his goodbyes, before leaving for the Far East, just a young soldier proudly wearing his new Army uniform.

Irene's next memory about him is as a nine-year-old, of coming home from school and of her father, Charles, showing her Joseph's picture on the front page of the *Daily Record* newspaper, featuring the story of his gallant action, and of feeling so sad, that she would never again see her cousin 'Josie'.

As a child, she would visit Joe's mother and father, at Pollockshaws Road; she always knew them as Aunt Sadie and Uncle Jack, and they would proudly show Irene Joe's George Cross medal in its special box.

Irene did well at school and, as a teenager, she worked part-time selling ice-creams in two local cinemas. When finishing school, she became a secretary for a local building contractor. Her Church and faith were always important to her and, at that time, she saved hard to be able to fulfil her dream to go on a pilgrimage to Lourdes in France. This, she happily achieved, although, in the mid 1950s, it was a tiring marathon of a four-day bus journey each way!

Like most teenagers of her era, she loved popular music and to dance. With friends she attended the local dance halls, the Pally and Locarno, and, like so many of her Hughes family, she had a lovely singing voice. She also enjoyed the social events at St. Margaret's Church, and there, on one auspicious day, she met young Tommy Finn and they fell in love. In September 1959, at the age of 22, they married at St. Bridget's Church, Toryglen, and were destined to have a happily fulfilled marriage, that was to last well over fifty years. Good long years of family love and fun.

Irene and Tommy's wedding, 1959

Irene and Tommy, September 1959

They first lived in Slead Street, Glasgow, and when they had outgrown it there, they moved on to Abernethy Drive in Linwood, Renfrewshire, where Tommy had by then got a job at the Rootes car factory. Rootes had moved up to Linwood and opened up in the early 60s, making the new rival to the mini, the Hillman Imp, which ended up bringing about its downfall. Linwood, not far from Paisley, was to be their home for the rest of their lives, together with their family of five children: Tony, Charles, Teresa, Carol and Martin.

Life was full and happy, but busy. For many years, Irene worked as a spinner at Coates Ferguslie Cotton mill until 1980, when they discontinued women working on the night shift. She then went on to be a dinner lady at Linwood High School, a job she loved, happy being around the many children there.

As the family grew up, they took local Scottish camping holidays and, later, they would often go to her and Tommy's favourite town of Blackpool, where they had honeymooned in 1959. All enjoying walking together along the famous Golden Mile, eating fish and chips, sometimes just to keep their hands warm! Lots of shopping and strolling out in the evenings, being entertained by the wonderful, colourful flashing illuminations, plus all the thrills of the sea-side!

There is a favourite family story of that time, of when, on their honeymoon, the second day there, they were surprisingly joined for the week by her holidaying Mum, Dad and her brothers, Charlie and Kenny, too!

Family life continued happily on, with children, weddings and grandchildren to enjoy. Later, as the years went by, with children grown up and left home, it became just her and Tommy taking Scottish holiday bus trips, sometimes to England, Ireland, Wales. or even venturing abroad to France or Germany.

But, for her and Tommy, their faith was important to them and the Catholic Church played a large part in their life. She played an active part in the Mothers' Union for many years and supported various charities close to her heart, enjoying reading their publications cover to cover and taking cuttings to share their stories with others who might be interested.

In the 1990s, Irene and Tommy were at the age, when they were beginning to think about retirement. Irene's thoughts also turned more and more to the past and to her cousin 'Josie'.

Over the years she had often gone to George Square in Glasgow city centre to place a small cross for Joseph in the Garden of Remembrance there. She had thought how little known his story was in his home city of Glasgow.

Irene had always been very proud of her special cousin, and so, one day, she decided to do something positive about it.

1996 Her quest for recognition for Joseph begins

Now, the years of Irene's prolific letter-writing began in earnest and stemmed from her desire for some kind of recognition for Joseph's gallantry by the City of Glasgow. She had thoughts of a road named after him or, a plaque placed somewhere in his home district of the Gorbals.

She first went to Edinburgh Castle to look at the Roll of Honour in their National War Memorial. She finally found his name in the Post War Casualty Book. It just contained the simple words: 'Joseph Hughes. Royal Army Service Corps. Died Hong Kong March 23rd 1946.' Nothing else, and no mention of his subsequent award of the George Cross in 1947.

High time, therefore, to write her first letter to try and get Joseph his due recognition.

Firstly, to the Edinburgh Castle curator, who passed it on to Army HQ In Scotland, who, in turn, passed it on to the head of Regimental HQ Hong Kong. Who then replied with a letter, enclosing information and photographs of Joseph's grave. He also said he would be contacting the Corps Regimental Secretary, Col J.D. Fielding, in Deepcut Barracks, Surrey.

This was a good beginning, but all then went quiet.

Over the next few years, she wrote to anyone who she thought could help her:

The Scottish Division of the RASC;

The *GorbalsLive* website to enter Joe's name on their site 'Roll of Honour';

The Archdiocese of Glasgow;

The City of Glasgow Planning Department;

The Lord Provost of Glasgow.

All politely replied and expressed interest, but she found that, with these potential contacts, things go extremely slowly.

However, her letter-writing campaign began to bear fruit. She did begin exchanging letters with the Royal Logistic Corps Regimental Secretary, Col J. D. Fielding, at Deepcut Barracks Museum, Surrey with the purpose of keeping them up to date with their archive of Joseph.

March 1996. Irene's first local newspaper story

It was the 50th anniversary of Joseph's Gallantry. His story was featured in the *Glasgow Sunday Mail*.

It was the report of a memorial tribute service to be held in Hong Kong by his regiment at Lyemun Barracks. It also said that here in Glasgow, his cousin, Irene Finn, would be attending a small service in her local Catholic Church.

After the excitement of the first local newspaper story and news of the memorial service in Hong Kong, all fell quiet again for a few years. In 2001, however, Irene was to have further success in her campaign. She got Joseph's name and his story added to a *Scots at War* website.

More than that, they added the following: "He is also remembered in the Gorbals area, where he lived and, due to the dedication of Irene Finn, his cousin, he is also remembered on the *GorbalsLive* website.

The research assistant also wrote personally to Irene, congratulating her for her 'excellent crusade' on Joseph's behalf.

Irene's quest was gaining momentum! People were at last beginning to listen.

A big milestone in Irene's dream!

Friday 23rd March 2001.

This was the time when two articles appeared in successive weeks in the Glasgow press, and Irene's campaign took a bit of a leap forward. First, on Friday 23rd March, there was a full-page spread in the *Glasgow Evening Times* on Irene's campaign to gain recognition for Joseph in his home city of Glasgow.

'One Woman's Battle over a Brave Soldier'

'Time to honour a forgotten hero'

Less than a week later, on Thursday 29th March, again in the *Evening Times*, there was a shorter story on the issue, concentrating on the supposed plans by the Safer Gorbals Initiative to honour the local hero, after seeing the previous full-page spread the week before.

It gets better and better for Irene! And another new friend for her and Tommy!

For, the second article in the *Evening Times* owed something to the intervention of Capt. Andy McArthur, the secretary of the Glasgow RASC and RCTA Association. Irene had been exchanging letters with him and received a letter in reply, with the most promising suggestion yet.

It had stated that he had written to Association HQ, to request instructions regarding a memorial for Joseph. He went on to say: "I am unable to make any promises, but please be assured, I will do my utmost to see it is done."

22 EVENING TIMES Friday March 23 2001

ONE WOMAN'S BATTLE OVER A BRAVE SOLDIER

JOSEPH HUGHES, the youngest Scot to be awarded the George Cross, is virtually unknown in his home city. On the eve of the 55th anniversary of his selfless death, JAMES HASTINGS reports on new moves by the Glasgow teenager's descendants to mark his sacrifice with a permanent memorial.

UNIQUE TRIBUTE: Joseph Hughes' grave in Hong Kong marking the day he died to save others and become youngest holder of the George Cross

Time to honour a forgotten hero

OLD men still tell stories about him in Hong Kong's smoking bars and young children place flowers on his grave.

Every year on the anniversary of his death, local people, many of whom owe their lives to his courage, stand in silent tribute around the memorial high on a hillside dedicated to Joseph "Jock" Hughes.

They gather to honour the teenager who was born thousands of miles away in the Gorbals and whose selfless bravery one fateful day saved the lives of hundreds of his comrades and villagers living near his barracks.

But while Joseph, the youngest Scot ever to be awarded the George Cross, may be a hero on the other side of the world, he is virtually unknown in his native city.

Over the decades, little had been recorded in official files about his bravery and there was only the briefest of mentions at the Scottish War Museum at Edinburgh Castle.

Even a new Gorbals website which commemorates local legends such as boxer Benny Lynch and architect Alexander "Greek" Thomson had no information on the young man.

Shocked by this, Joseph's cousin, Irene Firm, 64, from Linwood, who was only nine when her "big pal Josie" died, has launched a one-woman campaign to resurrect the memory of one of Glasgow's finest sons.

In a special plea through the Evening Times on the eve of the 55th anniversary of his death, Irene has called on the city to nominate a suitable memorial.

Joseph was just 19 and in the army for only a few months, when he was killed. He was driving a vehicle loaded with live ammunition and explosives when a fire suddenly broke out.

Without thinking of his own safety, Joseph guided the vehicle away from a convoy of other munition trucks then jumped on the back to tackle the blaze.

Even though the fire extinguisher failed and his clothes caught fire, Joseph fought on until the vehicle finally exploded in a huge fireball.

However, his actions gave enough time to evacuate his comrades and alert villagers in houses near the camp.

CAMPAIGNING: Irene Finn

"All those who were there that day realise how close they came to being killed," says Irene, 64.

"Joseph's truck was at the front of the convoy of vehicles loaded with ammunition and if he had simply run for cover, the explosion would have set off a chain reaction which would have devastated the highly populated area."

Joseph had been conscripted into the 387th Company of the Royal Army Service Corps early in 1946. The likeable lad was well known in the Gorbals and would proudly walk around showing off his uniform.

Irene added: "I remember Josie, as I called him then, coming over to my house with that great big smile of his and picking me up in his arms.

"He was always helping old people living on their own and playing with us kids. His mum was relieved the war was over and believed her son would be safe doing peacetime duties, and when he was posted overseas, we all went round to wave him off."

Joseph was sent to the Lymum Barracks in Hong Kong where he helped the war crimes commission in its search for unmarked graves as well as clearing land mines.

He was popular with people in the village neighbouring the barracks and had a knack of entertaining children despite the language barrier.

In fact, he was held with such affection by locals, that when he died, they asked to have him buried in their own cemetery rather than the military one.

"Josie was the only soldier in Hong Kong who was honoured in this way", explains Irene. It is a fitting tribute from the people who owed so much to this big lad from the Gorbals, a place I'm sure they'd never even heard of until Joseph arrived and told them all about Benny Lynch and others.

> I would still like his memory to be honoured in his home town
>
> IRENE FINN

"The cemetery is called the Happy Valley and is immaculately kept. I have been sent photographs and it looks lovely.

"There is also a memorial to him at the site of the former barracks which is now a holiday camp. Local people still talk about him today."

IRENE and husband Tommy, 66, moved to Linwood where they raised a family of four.

But in her mind all those years was a plan to find out everything she could about her cousin.

"I've spoken to practically every army division and to everyone from privates to generals," she laughs.

"I have to say everyone, especially Joseph's regiment, have been wonderful in helping my search.

"His George Cross was passed to the Royal Army Service Corps and is now on show at their museum in Surrey. They are very proud of it, as it is the only one the division has ever been awarded."

Irene fought to have Joseph's name added to the Scots War Roll of Honour as well as the new Gorbals website alongside other local legends such as Benny Lynch and Alexander 'Greek' Thomson.

In her quest to keep Joseph's memory alive, she has written to everyone from Cardinal Thomas Winning to the Lord Provost.

Recently she was proud to discover Joseph was commemorated on a special First Day Cover to mark the 50th anniversary of the George Cross.

"I cried when I saw it because it is such an honour. Josie would have hated the fuss but it is a fitting tribute."

Now Irene says her years of making sure Joseph would not be forgotten are at an end.

"I would still like his memory to be honoured in his home town and especially the Gorbals.

"If anyone has a spare street or a trust in the area which is looking for a patron, I hope they regard Joseph 'Jock' Hughes' as a suitable candidate."

In the meantime, the people of Hong Kong will gather today as usual to mark the 55th anniversary of the death of Joseph.

While the British may have pulled out of Hong Kong in 1997, there is one quiet corner in an immaculately trimmed cemetery high on a hill which will forever be a part of the Gorbals.

Photograph of *Glasgow Evening Times* Article (with permission)

Family joy over memorial

Gorbals will honour war hero Joseph

JOY: Irene Finn, left, and, above, how the Times broke the story of Joseph's heroism, which prompted moves to honour him in his native Gorbals

By Scott Russell

A GLASGOW soldier who became the youngest Scot to be awarded the George Cross is to be honoured in his native Gorbals.

Joseph Hughes was only 19 when he was killed after the ammunition lorry he was driving burst into flames and exploded.

The brave teenager managed to steer the vehicle away from his barracks and a nearby village saving the lives of hundreds of people.

Now 55 years after his death, a plaque commemorating his bravery is to be unveiled near the street where he grew up.

The Safer Gorbals initiative plans to honour the local lad, who died while serving in Hong Kong, after reading about his story in the Evening Times.

Today Joseph's cousin Irene Finn, who was only nine when he was killed in 1946, said she was "overjoyed" at the move.

She added: "Sadly, while Joseph is still well known today by the people in Hong Kong, he is largely forgotten about in Glasgow.

bravery and memory marked in some way and this idea seems just right.

"Joseph was born and bred in the Gorbals and very proud of it."

Since the Times told Joseph's story, we have been inundated with calls from old soldiers and friends who knew him.

Ian Cameron from Glasgow called to say he trained with the Gorbals teenager.

He added: "Joseph was a great lad. I'm delighted he is at last going to be remembered in a proper way."

Andy McArthur, a member of the Royal Army Service Corps said the unit welcomed the move and added the unit also planned their own tribute.

Jackie Murray, of the Safer Gorbals body, said: "When I read about Joseph Hughes I immediately knew he was a true hero.

"What he did was remarkable and we need to ensure other people never forget."

Jackie said she hoped a plaque near Joseph's birthplace in Pollokshaws Road, which has since been demolished, or a...

'Family Joy Over Memorial'. *The Evening Times*.
(With permission, *The Evening Times*)

Indeed, the Commanding Officer of the Glasgow Association had conveyed the request to his Commanding Officer, Lt Col David Owen at Deepcut Barracks. And he was then instrumental in producing a framed tribute to Joseph; a glass-fronted box containing, in the centre, a facsimile of his George Cross with a photograph of Joseph sitting on the bonnet of his truck. There was also one of his grave in Happy Valley and one of his memorial stone at the site in the old Lyemun Barracks, with a tribute inscribed beneath. This was forwarded to the Glasgow Commanding Officer of the Transport Regiment Association.

June 2002. A big step towards her dream!

All these wonderful developments had taken nine months or so, and all had resulted from the timely intervention of Irene's new friend, Capt. Andy McArthur. Consequently, at the Gorbals Fair, in the St. Francis Centre, Irene was officially presented with this framed tribute to Joseph by Lieutenant-Colonel C. J. Wensley, the then Commanding Officer of the Scottish Transport Regiment Association.

Irene then passed it on into the care of the Royal Army Service Corps and the Royal Corps Transport Association (Glasgow), who were in correspondence with Glasgow Councillor, Jimmy Mutter, hopefully to have the tribute mounted in future at the planned new Gorbals Library.

2002. Another new friend for Irene and Tommy!

At this time, Irene received a copy of the 1990 50th anniversary First Day Cover with Joseph's story on the front. It was gifted to her by former RASC soldier Bob Todd from Surrey, who had been a friend and army comrade of Joseph's, and had been at his military funeral in Hong Kong. He had heard about Irene's quest for a memorial for Joseph, the letters they exchanged leading to a lasting friendship between them, and subsequent visits to each other's homes and meetings at Deepcut Barracks.

New official contact with the army took place, with Irene supplying the regimental association with more letters and

22nd June 2002
Saint Francis Centre

Gorbals Fair Day hundreds step out to enjoy

Irene Finn and Andy McArthur with the plaque and replica of Joseph's medal

Honour for George Medal hero Joe

BEFORE the formal opening of Fair Day, a special ceremony took place to honour a Gorbals man who died a hero in Hong Kong in 1946.

Driver Joseph Hughes was given the George Cross, posthumously, for driving his blazing ammunition truck out of the way of the rest of the convoy and of the civilian population before it exploded.

Chief Lt Colonel Craig Wensley, R.L.C. commanding officer of the Scottish Transport Regiment which has a squadron based at Polmadie Road, told what happened and how two days after the blast, 19-year-old Joseph died from his injuries.

He told the respectful crowd: 'He is buried in Hong Kong at the request of local people, who remember him to this day and pay annual homage at his grave.'

Happy

He handed over a replica of the George Cross in a presentation frame with pictures of Joseph and a copy of his citation to Irene Finn, his cousin.

Irene said: 'It is a great honour to accept this on behalf of my cousin, his family, friends and comrades in the Royal Army Service Corp.

'I am very happy this will be displayed in Gorbals where he was born and brought up and I thank you from the bottom of my heart.'

After the moving ceremony, Mrs Finn said: 'I was 9 when Joseph died. We used to go to his mum's house and she'd show us the George's Cross.

'As the 50th anniversary of his death approached, I felt I wanted to do something to remember him.' She discovered a one-line mention of his death in the casualty book at Edinburgh Castle.

Eventually, she was assured by the present commanding officer of the Corp that Joseph's bravery was not forgotten, but was well documented as part of the regiment's history.

He had photographs of Joseph's grave in Hong Kong taken specially for Mrs Finn and sent to her.

But Mrs Finn wanted a lasting memorial in Joseph's birthplace. The commemorative frame was made with the help of the Evening Times, Andy McArthur, secretary of the Glasgow and West of Scotland Branch of the RASC and RCT Association and the Royal Army Service Corp.

Mrs Finn said: 'I feel wonderful. I've worked for six years to have a [illegible] memorial to Joseph in the G[illegible]bals and now it's happened.'

Councillor James Mutter said he was hopeful that the commemorative plaque would be hung in the Gorbals Library, Lifelong Learning Centre and Cyber Cafe when it opens next year.

Work on the building was expected to start at the end of June.

Irene Receiving Joseph Hughes GC Tribute. 22/06/2002.

photographs for their archives. The association secretary, Col J. D. Fielden, writing from Deepcut barracks, thought that it was wonderful that, after over fifty years, she had been able to generate so much interest and involvement of people in Joseph's home city. He thanked her for keeping them so well informed.

In her campaign, Irene had always enjoyed the full support and encouragement of her husband, Tommy. All the contacts Irene had made in her long, long fight for recognition for Joseph's heroism had brought with them many invitations for them both to attend special dinners and memorial services, giving them a whole new circle of friends. The whole time, Tommy was the rock Irene leaned on.

Irene and Tommy's Visit to Polmadie TA Open Day, April 2001

Irene as guest of Glasgow RASC, TA Association Service
Glasgow Cathedral, 2004

July 2003. A poem set to pipe music

Not long before then, her friend, Elsa Beattie, had written a poem of tribute to Joseph and Irene felt it should be set to pipe music, so she wrote an appeal for this in the *National Pipe Band Magazine.* An answer to her plea soon arrived from Pipe Major Pat Lee, who lived in Stamford, England. Her new friend had read her story and felt he would like to help.

True to his promise, in July 2003, he sent her a CD of his tune, part of it accompanied with drum. He wrote, hoping she liked it, saying he had composed it with the moving words of the poem in his mind.

Irene was thrilled, it was just as she would have wished, a slow lament on bagpipes and drum, to enhance Elsa's poem.

Col Fielden at Deepcut was most impressed by the music Irene had sent him and said he would send it on to the Regimental Pipers' Musical Director, as they still had a Piper at Deepcut Barracks. How pleased Irene must have been to receive his letter.

So, some you win, it seems, but, then again, some you don't! For Irene went further and offered the music to the Chief Executive Producer of The Edinburgh Tattoo, hoping for it to be played in its programme, as a tribute to Joseph. He politely declined, saying he did not think the Tattoo was a good location to do justice to such an important subject, but he did thank her for the idea!

You can listen to 'Driver Joseph Hughes GC' composed by Pipe Major Pat Lee (Stamford) and played on the pipe and drums by going to the following link on the internet. Alternatively, use a smartphone barcode/QR Code reader to access it directly on your smartphone:

https://archive.org/details/PipeTuneForJosephHughes

Tribute to Joseph Hughes GC.

Sheet Music 'For A Hero Was He'

'For A Hero Was He' by Elsa J Beattie

Joseph Hughes gave his life
For his Service Corps 'brothers',
His ultimate price
To save so many others.

Just a lad from the Gorbals,
How proud we should be
Of that brave young soldier,
For a hero was he.

His fear and his pain
We can only surmise,
How he must have suffered
In his sacrifice.

With esteem his name spoken,
As it always will be,
By his comrades-in-arms
Of the RASC.

In death then young Joseph
His actions rewarded,
For his gallantry,
A George Cross awarded.

His body lies cold
Far away in the earth.
But let's bring his soul home
To the place of his birth.

Each act of Remembrance
Brings Joseph back home.
To the 'Land of his Fathers'
His spirit will come.

So let's always remember,
With a thought or a prayer,
Joseph Hughes from the Gorbals
And his courage so rare.

Success at last. Ten Years Later!

In June 2004, there were two important developments. First, Irene received confirmation from the Scottish National War Memorial in Edinburgh Castle that Joseph's George Cross was being noted on the Roll of Honour. At long last, they had received confirmation from the VC/GC. Association in London. How slowly bureaucratic decisions are made!

Secondly, Irene was enhancing Joseph's memory with the VC/GC Association.

She received a letter from Didy Grahame, the secretary of the above Association, who said, as they were in the process of compiling a book on the lives and gallantry of all recipients of these illustrious medals, would Irene help them with the facts of Joseph's life? This, she was proud to do.

In May 2005, Irene and Tommy were invited to the VC/GC Association service of dedication at St. Martin's-in-the-Fields, London, to represent Joseph. Didy Grahame represented another important connection to add to Irene's growing collection.

And a painting of Joseph commissioned!

In 2004 Irene had commissioned a painting of the moment of Joseph's gallant action. It was painted by a well-known local Glasgow artist, Tam Smith. Tam is a self-taught painter and terracotta modeller, known especially for his models of parts of the old Gorbals.

After seeing the painting, Irene was absolutely delighted. She thanked Tam for his excellent painting, depicting Joseph's act of gallantry. Especially as he appears to have based it on the first day cover illustration, which had come out in 1990, and of which Irene had been given a copy, as we saw earlier.

Painting by Tam Smith

March 2006. Joseph's Memorial Sixty Years On.

Paddy and I were in touch with an author, Marian Hebblethwaite, who was researching and writing to publish a history of all acts of GC. Gallantry, the book to be entitled 'One Step Further'. She had contacted us for information on the life and story of our father, William Goad GC. During our correspondence, she realised our relationship to Joseph Hughes GC. and contacted us about a memorial tribute she knew was being held for him in Glasgow that March, which we knew nothing about.

Marian had heard of this event, as she was in contact with Irene, with regard to Joseph's story. Through these mysterious workings of fate, different people in our family story were slowly being drawn together.

We decided to go to Scotland to attend this service of remembrance and tribute. On the day, we still did not realise the key role she had been playing; we did not even meet her then. We were just pleased to be able to pay our personal tribute to our uncle's memory, and to meet Paddy's Scottish cousins, Angeline and Frank – Uncle Frank's children – for the first time in ages.

So, at this time we did not know of Irene at all, nor the work she had done to preserve Joseph's memory. This was because Paddy's parents, Bill and Sally, had died in 1988 and 1994 respectively, and news of the Glasgow family had not percolated through to us. With hindsight, we are so glad we were there, but it took nearly another ten years, before fate was to fit these pieces of our family jigsaw puzzle together.

For Irene her quest was over. Their City had given Joseph Hughes GC. a home in The St. Francis Centre, and permanent memorial for all to see.

She had, at last, succeeded in the desire that her 'Josie' would never be forgotten.

Cousin Frank with Connor and Mhairi; Cousin Angeleen and Steven; Paddy with wife Lesley and daughter Helen. St Francis Centre, 2006

Linking Cambridgeshire, Scotland and Australia

Closer links with our Glasgow family began to be restored, long after Irene's own heroic campaign, and soon after the idea of this book was born. That had arisen, after our Australian relatives had contacted us, having come across my earlier book, *Fen Farming Family*. Internet searches had connected us with long-lost family living on the other side of the globe. We needed to know more about our Scottish Hughes family, for Uncle James and his family, now that we were in contact with him in Australia. We had so many questions and few answers!

We contacted Marian to get Irene's phone number, and then proceeded to ring Irene in Scotland. We explained who we were and our reasons for contacting her. After talking a while, it was if we had always known her. We had a lovely chat and arranged to visit her that summer, when we were next in Scotland, visiting daughter Helen. Sadly, when this time came, Irene's husband, Tommy, had become ill, and it wasn't possible for us to see her.

Over the following months, Irene and I became 'pen pals' and also spoke on the phone at times, her happy letters and cards being always full of colourful butterflies and flowers. I then sent her a copy of *Fen Farming Family* with a version of Joseph's story in it, which I thought she would enjoy.

In her next letter of thanks, she said she had liked my book and asked if I would consider being her "Book Angel" and "fulfil her dream of Joseph's story being written for all to read in the future".

She also sent me a large package of cuttings, photographs and letters saved over many years, to encourage me! The rest is history as the expression goes.

I hadn't realised how ill her husband, Tommy, was and, sadly, he passed away in December 2015. By then, Irene, too, was very ill, although she continued sending her cheery little notes.

Therefore, knowing of her ill health, before we left for our planned visit to Australia the following March, I had sent Irene my ideas of the book she so dearly wanted written. Specifically, the idea I had of telling the story of how fate had linked us all at this time, and of her part in getting a memorial for Joseph. She replied, really liking my idea of combining the lives and stories of her two cousins with her in a family book.

March 2016, Joseph's 70th Memorial

Paddy and I flew out on our long-arranged visit to Uncle James and family in Australia. On the way, we stopped off in Hong Kong to lay flowers for the family on Joseph's grave in Happy Valley and visit his memorial. It was precisely on the same day as Irene attended his 70th Memorial Service at the St. Francis Centre with her family around her.

Irene with The Lord Provost of Glasgow

In our absence, Paddy and I were represented by his daughter, Helen, who took the photograph of Irene with the Lord Provost of the City. Helen was also representing Irene's cousin, James, from Australia. His daughter-in-law, Helen Hughes, had contacted Helen Goad, who was to lay a wreath on behalf of James and the Australian family.

It is entirely appropriate, that all the different branches of the family interacted, in full knowledge of all the facts, at what was to be Irene's last major appearance in public. To return once again to an oft-stated comment: fate, through Irene, had brought us all together.

Final words on Irene

Apart from seeing her at a distance, some ten years earlier, I was destined never to meet Irene. Her health had failed and, sadly, in September 2016, she too passed away. Almost until the end, we spoke on the phone and she sent me cheerful letters and cards with little facts she thought I might need. They always had beautiful butterflies on them, which she told me she believed were here as angels.

I felt I had lost a dear friend and so sad that she wouldn't see the finished book. And, above all, I felt so regretful that we hadn't managed to meet.

Paddy and I had driven to Scotland to be at her funeral and found we were so welcomed by her children and the extended Hughes family on that sad day, when they were all saying their fond goodbyes to such a special lady.

Tributes were written and read, which I have quoted from, to help me write this chapter and, hopefully, to enable me to do justice to the wonderfully giving, loving life she had enjoyed.

For the remainder of her life, a nine-year-old girl had kept in her heart those memories and that affection for her cousin, Josie. This had made it possible for me to tell the story of a love, that never dimmed, even through her years as a wife, mother and grandmother. For, this remarkable woman had always stayed constant in her determination to remind the people of Glasgow of the past courage of one of its sons, believing that it would set an example to future generations, and enhance their pride in the city of their birth.

Memories of Irene Hughes-Finn

The following sequence consists mainly of a photographic record of Irene, beginning with words spoken at the celebration of her life in September 2016.

> We cannot choose the way we die,
> Nor can we know the day.
> We only know there'll come a time,
> When we shall pass away.
>
> But we can choose the way we live,
> So when we do depart,
> We can leave a memory
> Of a good and caring heart.

Irene and Tommy

Teresa -Carol-Tony-Irene-Tommy-Martin-Charles, 1998

Musical Hughes
Irene and brother Kenny Hughes

Irene's father, Charlie and Uncle Jimmy

So ends the story of Irene and her long, long quest to secure recognition for Joseph Hughes GC in his home city. Thanks to Irene, the extended Hughes family has, in a mysterious way, been brought together around some of their shared heritage. As we saw, her final achievement was the placing of Joseph's memorial at the St. Francis Centre in Glasgow's Gorbals.

Now, at last, this story has been told for all to read. It stands as my personal tribute to a very special lady. What is more, this story of her dedication to the memory of her cousin, Joseph, will serve as her epitaph.

In her life, she touched many lives: I am so glad she touched mine.

Irene

Irene's Parents, Charles and Esther Hughes
With Bill McElhinney, 1937

First day cover commemorating Joseph Hughes GC

Painting of the blazing truck by Tam Smith

Painting of Ti Tree Road House

Paddy with family tribute at Joseph's grave.
Happy Valley Cemetery March 2016.

Hong Kong Memorial Dedication Service, March 22nd 2018

James Hughes laying a wreath, escorted by Graham Tomms

Christine and James Hughes, Chris Goad, Brigadier Robin Bacon,
Carole Goad and Graham Tomms.

New memorial to Joseph Hughes GC on the Hughes Dress Tartan

Chapter Four

James's Story – 'A Future Life Far Away'

James Hughes RN

Born 1924

James And Lucy Wedding Day, 1943

'A Future Life Far Away'

James Hughes was born 2nd August 1924. He was the first son of John and Sarah Hughes, born when his older sister, Sarah, was almost two years old. They were later to be joined by two more brothers, Joseph and Francis.

The little family grew up living at 159, Pollockshaws Road, in the Gorbals district of the City of Glasgow, with all the children attending St. John's Catholic Church and School, until they were fourteen.

As a child, James was a busy resourceful boy. He loved helping his father at work, and when he was collecting the seasonal fruits and tomatoes from local farms, which were to be taken by rail to city markets, the farmer often gave him baskets of split fruits and tomatoes, which he was thrilled to take home to his mother. He also collected used wooden boxes, which he chopped into kindling to sell in 1d bundles; he'd also wash neighbours' windows for 2d and collect old rags to cut up and sell to the 'rag and bone man'. He always enjoyed giving his mother the pennies, as life was hard for all families in the 1930s, at the time of the worldwide financial depression, mass unemployment and overcrowded housing of the Gorbals tenements.

James's first employment when he left school in 1938, was as a messenger boy for the Netherlee Co-op. He received 8/- a week, of which his mother gave him back 6d pocket money. When his wages went up to 10/-, he had 1/- to spend, which made him feel very rich. He was a big strong boy for his age and, when he was fifteen, he went to work as a labourer at an ammunition storage dump, run by a Mr Dawson from Manchester. He did long 12 hour shifts for 1/- per hour, and you could work seven days a week. At this job, mother returned to him 10/- for himself, he recalls that, at that time he was very proud to be able to help his family during such hard financial times and, as he could buy so much with his 10/-, he felt quite rich.

His mother, Sarah, was the unofficial local midwife, experienced and trusted by mothers to help in the birthing of their babies. She cared for new mothers, brought their babies into the world and knitted beautiful layettes for them. All this, she did with love and a big heart at this time of no National Health Service and when very few could even afford to call in the doctor.

He remembers seeing, as a boy, the renovation work being done on the old tea clipper ship, 'Cutty Sark', which, at that time, was in dry dock on the Clyde, before being taken to London, to be sited on the bank of the Thames for tourists to view. In its time, it had been the fastest ship to sail the world, swiftly bringing tea from China and wool from Australia to Britain. He also recalls seeing work being done on the famous engine, 'The Flying Scotsman', as the many working railway yards were behind Pollockshaws Road, where they lived, and where his father, John, worked. Lots of interests for a curious young boy!

James was very musical, as many of the Hughes family are. His mother and sister played the piano, and he would jostle with his enthusiastic older sister, Sally, to share the time they were given to play their mother's Fullertone piano.

Sally was very bright at school and sat in the top class in St. John's School for two years. Unfortunately, there was no chance of her being able to go on to further education at that time, but she used to like to help her younger brothers with their homework after school.

Their brother, Joe, was a good banjo player and used to busk in the streets on summer evenings and play football with his younger brother, Frank.

Music and singing were family evening entertainments, as were parties, especially at Christmas and Hogmanay, which were looked forward to. He always remembers his parents' favourite party pieces. Mother's was “When I Grow Too Old To Dream” and father's, “If You Were The Only Girl In The World.” How wonderful to be brought up in such a happy, singing, musical family.

He spent his childhood, with the army photograph of his father hanging on his bedroom wall, so, of course, it was quite natural for him to decide to join the local Army Cadets, as a piper, and play in their Pipe Band. As a teenager, he enjoyed spending his spare time learning all the Band skills of bagpipes and marching in time to a tune, until he achieved the rank of Pipe Sergeant Major.

He also loved dogs and had a black collie, called Lassie, who was his great pal.

After work, he used to like to pop and see his Aunt Esther, his Uncle Charlie's wife, who worked in the cake shop on Cumberland Street, and who would invariably give him spare cakes at the end of the day. These were his cousin Irene's parents.

James, Mum, Frank and dog, Lassie

Frank, James and Joe

In 1939, when James was fifteen, Britain declared war on Germany, when they invaded Poland, which was to be the start of the six long years of WWII.

James couldn't wait to go to war. A mature-looking boy for his age, he had tried twice to enlist as a marine, when he was under age, only to be discovered and stopped in time by his father. But, when turning eighteen in 1942, James joined the Royal Navy.

When James was having his enlisting medical, the navy doctor asked how he had acquired the substantial burns scars on his back. James knew nothing of them and, when he asked his mother, she told him he had, as a toddler, pulled the tablecloth from the table, causing a pot of scalding hot tea to spill on his back. She also said that, his good recovery, at that young age, convinced her that James was destined to lead a healthy, robust life.

As a young RN rating in training camp, when it was discovered by his officers he could march in time, thanks to having been Sergeant Major in the pipe band, he was immediately put in charge of training the new recruits on parade. For, James already knew that marching, or 'square bashing' as it is called, was an early skill, used to instil discipline in the ranks.

After his months of training, he was assigned to his first and only ship for the duration of the war, HMS Pheasant. This ship was to be his new home, and with it came the new name of Jimmy, given to him by his shipmates.

But, before being sent on his first voyage, he married his childhood sweetheart, Lucy Fletcher, a local girl he had grown up with and known all through his school years.

HMS Pheasant was a Black Swan Class Sloop, newly built on the Clyde in 1942, and, on completing its trails on May 12th 1943, it was commissioned for service in the 7th Escort Group.

Its first operational training took place in Irish waters and Scapa Flow, places his sailor brother-in-law, Bill, knew so well, too. James was then to join the 'Group' based in Greenock for escort duty with Convoy K MS 18 (operation Husky), supporting military convoys to the Mediterranean for the Sicily landings.

It was a whole new world of fighting and real-life war for the freshly-trained rating. His main duties on board were as a messman, working below deck, making sure strength and morale were maintained in all circumstances, with a good meal and hot cocoa, whenever needed.

Little did he realise how these practical skills he had learnt, would assist him so well in his later years.

HMS Pheasant was grounded off the coast of Tripoli, North Africa, and limped safely back home to port for repairs in the Clyde shipyard. This usually resulted in home leave, especially for local lads, giving some precious time for James to be with both his wife, Lucy, and his family.

At the end of September, they rejoined the 'Group' for Atlantic convoy escort to St. John's, Newfoundland, and, then, they escorted a returning UK Convoy. The need to get food and arms safely from America was paramount, as Britain was in the grips of rationing and shortages at that time.

James was very glad of his mother's knitting skills in this cold Arctic climate on board ship. She had supplied him with wonderful, warm hand-knitted polo-neck jumpers, gloves and sea boot socks. In war time, new wool had been scarce, so, she unpicked old jumpers, washed and re-knitted the wool, lovingly recycling it back to him with garments as new.

In November 1943, they were sent to the Mediterranean and, on passage to Gibraltar, HMS Pheasant came under attack, off the coast of Portugal, from a group of German U-Boats. She survived, but limped back into dock for a refit in Newport, South Wales. By then, it was December 1943, and, so, one might have hoped that, after his adventure, James would have been able to have Christmas at home with his family. Luckily, he managed to get home for the all-important Scottish New Year Hogmanay.

But, on finding himself short of cash for the long train journey back home to Glasgow, he was glad he had had the foresight, when he was in dock in North Africa, to put on board in the hold, large bunches of green bananas. These were now ripe and yellow and as scarce as gold in those times of rationing! He took a big bag of them with him to barter for his train and bus fares, and found he had no trouble getting home. He even had bananas left over for a special treat for the family, too.

On board ship, James never drank his 'Splice the Mainbrace' daily ration of strong 'Pussers' rum, served up by the ship's purser. Not being a great alcohol drinker, he saved each tot in a port wine bottle to take home to his parents. So, he arrived home that New Year, bottle in hand, and presented it to his father. John, thinking it was port, took a drink, choking in surprise at the strength of his first sip. Pausing, and after a little thought, he decided it should be put away for mother and him to drink for 'medicinal purposes'!

Much to James' s amusement!

By February 1944, HMS Pheasant was back in Gibraltar to join Group convoy escort between Gibraltar and Port Said, Egypt. After eight months service in the busy Mediterranean, October found him back in Leith, Scotland for another refit.

HMS Pheasant

Ship's emblem

James and shipmates in 'whites'

No Christmas at home, though, and in December 1944, HMS Pheasant was back in Gibraltar, needing more repairs, as their deployment had changed. The war on the Far Eastern Front with Japan was in great need of reinforcements and, on 13th January 1945, they took passage via The Red Sea, and on to Darwin to join the British Pacific Fleet for escort duty operations in the S.W. Pacific, arriving, in March 1945, at the Fleet Base at Manus Island.

Until May, he was on defence convoys with British Fleet Replenishment ships, providing air defence, and they later escorted Royal Australian Navy warships during the continuation of joint Royal Navy and US Navy operations against Japanese targets in Sakishima-Shoto Islands by Task Force 57.

By June, the ship needed more maintenance and docked in Darwin, Northern Australia, where they had a substantial leave period. This long, enjoyable visit to Darwin was to leave a significant impression on James, as we shall see later in his life.

A month later, when back on duty at sea, his Captain sent for him and informed him that he was being given immediate compassionate leave to return home to Scotland, as his wife Lucy was very ill.

The next amazing story of this eventful solo trip of James's from Manus Island back to Scotland was written by James himself in 1995, fifty years later and printed in his ship's association magazine, 'The Pheasant Echo', in England.

The Pheasant Echo header

"Perils in the Pacific 1945"

By Jimmy Hughes

Chapter One

"I Am Marooned!"

We were sailing on HMS Pheasant on our usual erratic course on the bosom of the unbelievably blue Pacific Ocean, day after day, boring day after boring day, as Senior Officer of the Fleet Train Escort in support of The British Pacific Fleet in the year of 1945, when one day the Captain sent for me and informed me, rather alarmingly, that there was an emergency at home, and that I was to be sent back home forthwith.

Hurriedly packing up my gear, I reported on the upper deck to face the ordeal of transfer from ship to ship by breeches buoy. The necessary equipment was rigged up, and I was preparing to entrust my life to a piece of rope, when an Australian mail ship came alongside. My bag and hammock were passed down to her, followed by myself. I was taken back to an island and put ashore, but I never knew the name of this island!

All alone, I left my bag and hammock on the beach and walked inland for a spell to report to a Yank Army Camp. They did not take too kindly to me, as I was completely foreign to them, dressed as I was in Royal Navy tropical rig of white shirt and shorts! In fact, they thought I was French, and put me in a tent under guard!

But I did not realise that I was being guarded, until I wanted a drink of water. I could see a tap outside and made to leave to get a drink – but was smartly put back in my tent 'prison' at the point of the sentry's gun!

I did not blame them at all, as I must have been a most unusual sight, appearing out of the jungle in my strange garb and my Scottish accent, not easily understood by them. After all, they were soldiers fighting a war. But, after a while, I was sent for as they had picked up my gear from the beach, and in it I had a letter signed by Admiral Bruce Fraser, no less, requesting all concerned to facilitate me in a speedy passage back to Britain. So, after a bit of communication was done, I was at last set free.

A day or so after this 'break-through', I was sent on an open US Army barge to another island some distance away. Indeed, it was quite a journey. There were other US Servicemen in this barge, and there was no cover from the sun. Me being in short sleeves and pants, I was getting badly sunburned. I managed to team up with a couple of friendly Yank sailors on the journey. When we arrived at our destination, it was getting late, and we were directed to the Dining Hut for a meal, but I ran into more trouble, when a guy at the entrance would not let me enter, he said, 'You can't come in here dressed like that!' He meant my shorts of course.

My new-found Yank naval friends came to my rescue by explaining to the sentry that this was my uniform and that I was on their side! But the sentry would not budge, and insisted I wore long pants, before I could go in. So, one of my new sailor mates opened his bag and found me a pair of his I could wear, and a shirt to match, so I was, at last, allowed in to the hut for a meal. I cannot remember, but it was Spam, no doubt!

I wore this US Navy gear for quite a while and found it much easier to get around so attired, although I kept my Navy cap on, so I wasn't altogether a 'gob' (US Slang for sailor) and my paperwork really worked. I presented it, whenever I arrived anywhere, and was usually accepted. Each place, I had to wait for transport heading in the direction I wished to go, and found that the Yanks were very good at moving me on quickly. Eventually, I arrived at an island called Samar and put on board a large Depot Ship!

After the island hopping this was great and, as I stood on deck in the evening on a lovely tropical night, I could hear music coming from below decks. It was 'The Andrews Sisters' singing 'Rum and Coca Cola'.

This has always stuck in my mind.

Chapter Two

"In the Best Company Plus A Confession"

In the last chapter, I had reached Samar in the Philippines and was billeted in a depot ship. The next part is hazy, but, somehow or other, I landed next on Letye, from where I was transported in some style across the Pacific to Honolulu in the Hawaiian Islands. I can remember the first-class Nave Barracks, double-storied and spotlessly clean, and the food was quite amazing, after what we had been used to. The Yanks gave me some American Dollars, so I was able to buy some odds and ends from their canteen – plus some clean clothing, which was a great blessing, I can tell you!

I must have spent nearly a week there. As I kept no diary, everything is from memory.

When I did leave Honolulu, it was on a VIP plane – no, not for me! This plane was heading for the States and carried numerous VIPs, as President Roosevelt had just died, and his son was on board, plus other high-ranking officers, going on to Washington and the funeral.

The plane with its valuable cargo arrived in San Francisco, where security was understandably tight. Everyone was put through a diligent Customs search – and here I must apologise to some half-dozen shipmates from Pheasant – as I was leaving the ship bound for the UK. Then, naturally, some of our mates took the opportunity of having some mail for home delivered or posted in UK. I was carrying quite a few letters and noticed that the Customs men in San Francisco were opening just about everything they found – and so, boys, whoever you were, I am sorry to say that I took your letters outside and tore them up into small pieces!

Then I was taken to a US Navy Barracks in Frisco, and there I stayed for another few days – but I will leave Frisco until the next chapter.

Chapter Three

"Adventures in The New World"

I was in the Naval Barracks in San Francisco for 3 or 4 days, waiting for transport heading my way – a sort of aerial hitch-hiker – although I can't remember what I did there. I suppose, being Royal Navy, they did not know what to do with me, and so I had a cushy time of it. Eventually, I was summoned by Authority and found myself on a plane heading deep into the heart of Texas (A good title for a song!)

Such planes, by the way, were not the luxurious airliners of post-war, but were truly maids of all work, carrying mail, goods, sundry service passengers – and no stewardess service either! I remember landing at a mainly civilian airport in Texas, where I had to wait, yet again, for another convenient lift. I tried to buy myself a cup of coffee and a sandwich, but no American money left. I had all sorts of currency, although not a lot, including English, Australian, and some odds and ends like piastres, rupees, Hawaiian, but none acceptable in the Land of the Silver Dollar, so I had to go hungry.

Fortunately for me, I left Texas that night on a plane, where I had a seat to sit on, instead of a mail bag, and my next stop proved to be Washington DC. Once there, at the airport, I headed for the Transport Desk, it was either Navy or Air Force, where I showed my papers and tried to get them to keep me moving, as I found by experience that, when I landed at any sort of barracks or depot, I was invariably held up for a few days. But this time I was lucky and was on my merry way again in no time, complete with bag, hammock, and ditty-box.

My next stop was New York City, where I had a very pleasant surprise. When I approached the Transport Desk, the Petty Officer (US Navy, of course) listened to my story and then said the magic words, "When did you eat last?" When I told him, he immediately wrote out a chit and told me to go to the Dining Hall. "It's closed, but give them this chit and you will be fixed up. When you are ready, come back and see me." I will never forget that man. A simple gesture, but it made me feel great.

After a much-needed meal, I duly went back and saw the PO, who had already made arrangements for me to be transported to Brooklyn Barracks – where I made contact once again for the first time since leaving HMS Pheasant in mid Pacific!

Chapter Four

"Further Adventures in The New World"

At the end of the last chapter, I was on my way to Brooklyn Barracks, New York, and my first contact with the Royal Navy since leaving HMS Pheasant at sea, somewhere off Okinawa. It was evening before I arrived, and I reported to the Officer of the watch or PO, I forget which. Naturally, they knew nothing about me, and after a lot of talk and explaining, I was given a bunk for the night.

In the morning, I was sent for, and I was in for a shock as I was 'put on the mat', 'Off Caps' and all, and was given the third degree, questioned about the Pheasant, my travels, and everything else they could think of. It was a bit of a worry at the time, as I did not think I had done anything wrong. The officer doing the questioning was quite tough in his approach to me and asked me about my stop-overs, and how I had managed to obtain onward passage. I told them all I could to the best of my ability.

Then I was asked, "Do you realise that you were supposed to have reported to the authorities here, there, and everywhere – and at Washington DC?"

I replied I had no knowledge of this, as my papers from Captain Palmer stated that I should find my way home by the quickest possible route, and that assistance was to be given me by travel personnel. Upon reflection, I do not think I was very popular in that office. Finally, I was dismissed and put on duty (on the 'EMU' Squad), picking up paper and cigarette-ends on the parade ground. I think I was being punished, although for what, I could never understand!

Eventually, after my shock re-entry into the arms of the Royal Navy, I settled down to a normal routine, being put on guard duty and the usual barracks work. I soon made mates with a few of the ratings there, and it was a good thing for me to be able to talk to sailors, who spoke the same sort of English as I did!

When I think back on my interrogation, I now realise that I was being checked out to see if I was, in fact, who I claimed to be. After all, the war was still on. So, they did right in clearing my story. I must have been in Brooklyn Barracks well over a week, as I can remember going 'ashore' on at least four occasions. By this time, I had a new mate, so we went ashore together. I wanted to look around New York, so we did a lot of walking around the shops, which, in itself, was a novelty to me, as they were so well stocked with goods, which we looked on as luxuries.

I went into one shop to buy something, probably a souvenir, to take home, but I was puzzled by the pricing system. If the price of an article in the window was, say, 10 dollars, the assistant inside the shop asked me for 12 dollars 50. I baulked a bit, "But in the window it says 10 dollars?" "Oh yes," they said, "but plus tax it's 12.50." I did not buy the article, as I did not understand the dollar system and had to convert to Sterling to find out how much it would really cost me (you know, in real money!) This selling in prices plus tax put me right off, as, not being a millionaire, I had to watch the dollars and cents!

We continued our run ashore, and I stood looking up at The Empire State Building, saw Times Square, and the theatres. My 'going-ashore mate' acted as my tour guide, as he had been there a while, which was lucky for me.

My next run ashore was more exciting. I had heard about the Stage Door Canteen, and wanted to go there, so we did. It was a great experience and the whole atmosphere was great. The place was naturally filled with servicemen, and we could buy drinks and snacks, and the entertainment was fantastic – the stars who were performing in the theatres on Broadway gave up a bit of their time to perform in The Canteen. You may remember a record the Yanks used to play on their Forces Network, it was a song sung by a girl named Lily Anne Carol, and was called "I'll Walk Alone". The Yanks used to announce her as 'Lily – I'll Walk Alone – Carol'.

Well I had the pleasure of seeing her at the Stage Door Canteen – and hearing her sing that song.

My third run ashore was not quite so exciting, still, it was good. We finished up at some sort of club, where servicemen go for the evening and have cups of coffee, a singalong, and a bit of dancing. The young ladies were under strict supervision – no mucking about!! The company was good and we had a pleasant time.

The fourth shore run was quiet, as we went to the movies, although I can't remember what we saw, but I do remember what we met on the way back to barracks!

My mate and I were standing on the platform of the subway, waiting for our train, when we were approached by a Yank, who got into conversation with us and seemed friendly. He told us he was going our way and lived near the barracks, and invited us home with him for a cup of coffee. But when we arrived at his flat, we soon found he was after more than conversation and coffee. My first real, live queer I'd ever seen!

My mate and I sat on the sofa at his request, and he was showing us photos and stuff, then his jewellery. He sat in the middle of the sofa and began putting his arms around us – we decided it was time for a quick exit, so we left and headed back to the safety of the barracks, having a bit of a giggle over this episode!

The next few days were quite hectic, and I was told to get my gear packed, as I was off on my travels again. I was to be sent to Canada by train! But that will have to wait until the next chapter.

Chapter Five

"I Say Goodbye to my Gear – And Hello to Montreal"

In Brooklyn Barracks, I was told to pack my kit and mark it well, then take it to the Stores, as I would not need my cumbersome kit-bag and hammock with me on this trip. I was a bit disappointed after carrying my gear more than halfway around the world. I was to leave it behind to be sent home by sea. Well, as you might guess, that was the last I ever saw of my bag and hammock. So, I lost all my 'rabbits', photos, and personal gear, and lots of memories, and was left to make do with a hand-held bag.

I was told to report to the RPO Office, where I was issued with a rail warrant and an itinerary telling me where to go and where to stay. I was given quite a large sum of Canadian dollars, as I had to pay my travel and accommodation expenses, and apparently there were no barracks or other military bases where I was going.

But back to my packing; I still had some American dollars left, so I thought I'd be cunning and spend them all here to prevent being stuck with them. So, off I went to the PX Store (as the Yanks call it. I think we call them 'Slops'), and waited in a queue to be served, and was busy sorting out my 'foreign' currency (meaning US Dollars).

I asked one of the 'gobs' (i.e. US sailors) if Hawaiian dollars were accepted in the store. His eyes popped out of his head as he had never left the USA and never seen Hawaiian money before, so he offered me twice their value. Soon, others gathered round and I had an auction going in no time at all. I soon had no more 'foreign' money left, and had made a handsome profit into the bargain, which I promptly spent in the PX. My first purchase was a hand grip bag, which I proceeded to fill with shirt, socks, underwear, shoes, knife, and just kept going until I had spent all my dough.

Next day, I was taken by car to Grand Central Station in New York, where I was left on my own once again. Bye bye Brooklyn Barracks! Grand Central was a very impressive place, very large and spacious, like a small town. I found my train for Canada. It was First Class, and most comfortable, nothing like the trains from Pompey to Glasgow. No standing in corridors or sitting on kit bags. We sat instead, in armchairs with passenger service by stewards, there were also First-Class Dining Rooms.

I met up with an English business-man (at least, that's what he said he was). He was very knowledgeable and made a good companion. He seemed to know his way around the States very well, so we had a good journey. We were both heading for Montreal, and he asked me where I was staying there, and I gave the name of the hotel shown on my travelling orders. He remarked that he stopped there, whenever he visited Montreal, so, when we arrived there early in the morning, my friend suggested that we share a cab, which suited me fine, as I had no idea where to go.

When we stepped out of the cab and made to enter the hotel foyer, I nearly saluted the magnificently uniformed doorman, who looked for all the world like an Admiral, medals and all! But this impressive figure meekly opened the door for us. I remember thinking, as we walked across this 'palace' floor of marble, cream and chrome, 'This is not for me!' But my friend seemed quite at home, as he signed the register. But I made an excuse to go outside, as I spotted an Airways booking office just outside the hotel. Sneaking past the 'Admiral' and going into the Airways office to enquire about the next flight to the UK, I was told nothing doing, and to keep in touch.

I explained to the man in the Airways office, that I did not want to stay in the 'plush' hotel next door, and asked if there were any YMCAs or other places a serviceman could lay his head, but was told they did not have such places in Montreal. He was a real nice chap, and understood my predicament, and rang a few cheaper hotels, less pretentious, and expensive than The Palace next door, but to no avail. Then he got onto some ladies auxiliary group, who made cups of coffee and such for servicemen passing through. Bingo! I was given directions to this place.

When I arrived, I found it to be like a canteen with volunteer ladies running it. Soon, breakfast was served to me, and I had the name of a lady to contact. This was the one the Airways office had spoken to. This kind lady made me very welcome and offered to accommodate me at her home, while I waited for a plane home. Her son was in the Navy and based at Greenock, Scotland, and so I had his room for about five days.

I offered to pay for my board and lodging from the money I had for the hotel, but she would not take it and suggested I spend it on clothing and presents for my family. So, with her help, we went shopping. I maintained contact with that kind lady for about five years after the war, with postcards at Easter and at Christmas.

Chapter Six

"Home At Last!!"

In Montreal, I am on the move again, heading for the airport. I cannot remember just how I was contacted or how I made my way to the plane. All I know is, that there I was, flying high across the Atlantic, looking down at the white horses for a change. It was certainly more comfortable than ploughing through those high waves.

That flight brought back a lot of memories, as I gazed down on this great expanse of wild water – and it did look wild! I thought of the times our little ship had to do battle with these elements and at times sustained storm damage.

But back up to the plane! I did not know exactly where we were heading, but, lo and behold, the aircraft landed at Prestwick, near Glasgow, my home town. There I was, my feet firmly planted on home soil at last. I had circumnavigated the world!

But my worries were not over yet. As I passed through the arrival gate, I was asked to show my Pay Book for ID. Horror of horrors – my photograph was missing!

That was no good, and I was taken aside to sign my name on a piece of paper – which I did. There was much shaking of heads, and glances towards me. I was then asked to 'Come this way' and taken into a room where, again, I was very closely questioned about my name, rank, service number and all sorts of things. They then phoned Portsmouth to check on me. I was detained for about four hours, before they decided to let me go, but I was to be shipped off to Portsmouth Barracks, about 500 miles away – and here I was, about 25 miles from home!

Back to the shaking of heads over my signature; the reason being, that I had changed my style of writing while I was on Pheasant. I had been given a gild signet ring by my mother, with my initials in fancy scroll writing, and, over the years, I had sort of copied that attractive scroll into my ordinary writing, so that my current signature was markedly different from the original signature in my Pay Book! I had spent hours on board Pheasant practising my new 'scroll-type signature', never thinking I was creating a problem for myself.

I remember asking the people at Prestwick to reconsider sending me back to Portsmouth, as I was travelling on compassionate grounds and was so near to home. More phone calls and I was told to report to a Naval Base in Glasgow's St. Enoch Railway Station, where I met the Personnel Officer, who had started the ball rolling, knew all about me and my reason for travelling. So, I was truly home now, was given a leave-pass and 14 days leave. So, that night I slept in my own room – AT LAST!

When my leave finished, I reported back to the same officer, who arranged that I be stationed in Glasgow, at St Enoch's Hotel, which the Navy had commandeered for their HQ. I was put on guard duty and, would you believe it, I was billeted at home, in my own house. I travelled from home to report for duty, and sometimes I would just walk into the hotel. We were watch keeping, so when I was on Middle or Morning Watch I stayed at the hotel, where we had a few bunks up in the attic for that purpose. It was a cushy job – standing at a desk in the corridor and giving directions to anyone who was lost. There were three floors with a sentry on each.

I cannot remember the exact date (but I am sure you all on the Pheasant will), I was on Morning Watch and was sitting back in my chair, about 6.30am reading the local paper, when there it was – Headlines: Glasgow-built ship among the first to enter Tokyo Harbour – HMS Pheasant – Clyde-built – and so on. The Pheasant was given a good write-up.

I felt a bit sad at missing out on this great occasion, in fact, I still do. I was very happy on board Pheasant and never really wanted to leave her, but circumstances decreed otherwise. St. Enoch's Hotel was my last posting in the Royal Navy.

The 'powers-that-be' had decided that they no longer required the hotel as a base. So, we were all put to work packing up and moving all Naval gear, furniture, etc. into storage.

I reported as usual one morning to take over my watch, and surprise, surprise, I was told by one of my mates that we were no longer required and that we were to be demobbed.

I could not believe him and made a few enquiries in more appropriate quarters. But, sure enough, we started demob procedure straight away, had a medical check and were given rail warrants to Edinburgh, where the Demob Centre was.

After the necessary formalities, we left Edinburgh, clad in our new Civvy suits, and that was the end of my Naval service in March 1946.

Postscript to James's Round-the-World Trip

Fate had taken a hand in James's life, for, as he said in his account, he had not been with his shipmates in Yokohama Bay on Sunday 2nd September, and he had missed the Japanese surrender. HMS Pheasant had been there all right, as part of a large flotilla of Allied shipping. And his shipmates stood on deck, watching through binoculars, this significant moment of world history.

And so had the Japanese government, resplendent in top hats and long, black coats, as they signed the armistice with the American Supreme Commander on the deck of the USS Missouri, in full view of James's former shipmates on the Pheasant.

Also, the ship's next assignment was to be Hong Kong, as part of the 32nd Escort Group, in defence of British shipping. Had James been on the Pheasant at that time, he would almost certainly have met his brother, Joseph, who was there by then. Fate had decreed otherwise, of course, and the fact that he had also missed Joseph in Hong Kong would always be a great regret for Jimmy.

HMS Pheasant was the only wartime ship James had sailed on and, consequently, he forged many long-lasting friendships in those times of war, with his comrades, who were never forgotten.

Jimmy Back Home in Glasgow

'Post-War Times'

James was back home in Glasgow, and happily, the crisis in Lucy's health had passed this time, but James knew she was frail. He was demobbed from the Navy in March 1946, and decided to take up the offer of the Government ex-servicemen's course to train as a carpenter.

Thankfully, he was home in Glasgow that March to help and comfort his mother and father through the emotional turmoil of losing his brother, Joseph. As we have already seen, this had been a difficult time for all the family.

James's love of carpentry was to serve him in good stead. He had rented a little house in Cavendish Road and, with his own skills and those of a few friends, he made a comfortable home for him and Lucy. But happiness wasn't to last for long. Sadly, Lucy passed away in 1948. She had talked to him of this day, knowing how poorly her health was, and encouraged James, next time around, to 'marry a girl who could run', as something she had never been able to do. It is hard to imagine the effect of this loss on James emotionally, on top of the recent events of losing Joseph. There was also the fact that Lucy had been part of his life from when they were children together, and was now leaving him a widower at the young age of twenty-four. He had only a few words to say about this, sixty-five years later, when I was talking to him of this time, but obviously many memories were too sad to want to recall. He spoke of taking his meals back home with his parents at Pollockshaws Road, the family being a comfort and support, and, as he always did, he kept working hard.

It was now the late 1940s, the post-war world was changing and the Labour Party was in government. It had introduced the revolutionary National Health Service with a revised old age pension, a new family allowance and also the nationalisation of the railways and coal mines. But, it was still a time of austerity, with many shortages of food and lots of rationing. All these new political social changes would to take years for everyone to begin to feel the benefits. But, always, it was a time of hope for all, of peace and new beginnings.

But James couldn't settle. In 1949, he eventually decided on a truly new beginning. As a young man, during war-time, he had seen may things. He had travelled the world and visited many countries. His life experiences had now given him choices and new horizons. He had thoughts of Canada or Australia. But, a few years before, as a young sailor on leave, he had visited Darwin, and remembered its people and warm climate with some affection. So, it would be Australia for him.

So, he sold the 'utility' furniture he and Lucy had bought to her sister, whose husband had recently been demobbed. Incidentally, he had just recovered in America, after having been released from a POW camp in Japan. This helped to give him the grand sum of £200 to begin his new life in Australia. He packed his personal belongings in a big trunk, his tweed suits and, most importantly, his collection of carpentry tools; his one sure way of earning a living.

Now to say his goodbyes!

At this time his young cousin, May Wogan, who regularly visited from her home in Ireland, was holidaying with his parents and, before he left, he took her out dancing. Little did they know that, a few years later, she was to become his sister-in-law, when, in 1956, she would marry his younger brother, Frank. At the time James emigrated, Frank was aged 22 and still living at home. He had not been called to serve in the Army, as he was in a reserved occupation, much to the relief of his parents.

James then visited all his Scottish family, and his sister, Sally, and her family in Stretham, Cambridgeshire, England, to say his goodbyes. And then, that November, he took his difficult final leave of his mother, his father and his young brother, Frank.

He told me he could remember to this day his father's final words of advice to him, before he left, which were: “Son, wherever you go, keep in with the cook!” Home-spun wisdom his Dad, John, had learnt from experience, but choosing words to disguise his feelings and to lighten the occasion, no doubt. How sad they must have been to see him go!

On 19th November 1949, James set sail on the Cunard Line Package Ship, The Ormond, to cross to the other side of the world to seek his fortune, to have unforeseen adventures and to fulfil his future life's destiny.

Australian Flag

Sketch map of Australia

Highlighted Places are mentioned in the story and many feature in Jimmy's future life in Australia

Jimmy's Australian Dream

The Ormond's voyage from Britain took eight weeks, travelling halfway around the world. Passage was free and no passport was needed at this time for ex-servicemen travelling to a British colony. It didn't take James long to find his sea legs; he relaxed and enjoyed being waited on for a change. It was the first real holiday he had ever had, revelling in lots of new experiences and meeting new people, some just like himself, travelling to a new world for a new life.

As he approached the port of Sydney with feelings of excited anticipation, he was eager to begin the unforeseen adventures, of which he had been dreaming back in Scotland, as a young man of twenty-five. It was a New Year when they docked, and the new decade of the 1950s.

From now on, I shall refer to James, as his Scottish family always called him, as Jimmy. For, that is the name he was known by, when in the Royal Navy, and that is what he has always been known as in all the years he has lived in Australia.

So, Jimmy, was about to begin this new, independent, adventurous era of his life.

After disembarking, he took a train to the capital city, Canberra, looking for work. He soon found he was busy, with many people needing his skills. One day he heard the tales about the possibility of finding gold, and decided he would also go prospecting in New South Wales, but, unfortunately, he had no luck with that!

He then heard there was work for carpenters near the Northern Territory at the town of Daly Waters, which is some 350 miles south of Darwin and some 570 miles north of Alice Springs, giving us a good idea of the sheer size of this new country Jimmy had found. So, Jimmy packed up his 'port', as his trunk was called in this 'new world' and, with his few treasured belongings, he set off north, on a trip by train, following the route of the old track of the Stuart Highway, through the unknown, endless, barren desert in the heart of the country.

Mining for gold, New South Wales, 1950

The train is today still called the 'Ghan', as a tribute to the early immigrants from Afghanistan, Pakistan, India and the Middle East, who were all known collectively as Afghans. In the mid-19th century, they had come with their camels and soon bred more in Australia. They also rode long camel trains through the heat and dust of central Australia, all the way from Adelaide to Darwin, and, as they went, they planted date stones alongside the trail, taken from the staple food they carried with them, which accounts for the date palms often now found growing there.

They also played a major role in constructing both the road and the railway across the vast, central desert. The great Stuart Highway itself was, and still is, a solitary bitumen ribbon road, edged with shingle, reaching from south to north of the country. It was built to enable large supply trucks, called road trains, to travel across the hot, barren, red, desert interior. And to take much-needed supplies across this empty terrain, their end destination being the port of Darwin, far away in the north.

The Government was building at Daly Waters a larger refuelling airfield for the increasing number of supply 'hop-planes' in this region since WWII, and houses for the workers there. To begin with, they lived under canvas or in rough makeshift shacks of old wood and tin. This life for Jimmy was a really new experience, learning to live and deal with the constant heat and dust, bugs and mites.

His workmates, like him, were men from all over the world, living together in a big work camp. It was his first time of working alongside the local Aboriginal population, he observed how they lived and their traditional culture. Seeing their beliefs and their survival skills, he realised that the way they thought and lived were the reasons they were still there after thousands of years. They were people he was later in his life to employ and live beside easily, thanks to all the knowledge he had soon picked up about them.

He became friends with Bill Pearce and his wife, who ran the Daly Waters Station. In 1945, a book had been published of their experiences there in the 1930s, as told by his wife, which immortalised their little station. A cameo of a time and place, this book was called *Two at Daly Waters*. It achieved great success all over the world, and, ultimately, it became part of Australian children's school curriculum.

After a year at Daly Waters Airfield, the building work was finished and it was time to move on. Jimmy then heard that, at the mineral mines further east, at Mount Isa, there was work for carpenters to build houses for the growing workforce there. Located in North Queensland, the mines were successfully producing zinc, lead and copper.

Mount Isa, at that time, was an isolated mining camp on a dry, dusty, desert plain, and was known as the 'oasis of the outback', as it appeared like a gleaming mirage on the horizon, to travellers approaching from all directions. It is over 700 miles north-west from the Queensland capital of Brisbane and, for Jimmy, it seemed a world away from his Scottish home, always in his mind.

When Jimmy was planning to move there, it was early 1951 and, due to the constant tropical heat, he decided he didn't need the many warm tweed suits he had brought with him, so, he packed a parcel to send back home to his brother, Frank, in Glasgow, which was gratefully received.

Jimmy had learnt so much about survival in this foreign terrain – dealing with the constant heat, winds, dust, drought and, then, with the tropical season of torrential storms. There was also the need to be vigilant of the strange, unknown species of predators, of spiders, ants, snakes and poisonous insects, which threatened everyday life. But, most importantly of all, you had always to keep fresh drinking water available. Jimmy took all of this in his stride. His hard-working, sunny nature saw him through many sticky situations.

To this day, he has a vivid memory of the journey to Mount Isa. After leaving the train at Alice Springs, he then travelled on a bus going east. He still recalls organising sing-alongs with the other passengers, with him solo-singing the then popular hit song 'On Top of Old Smoky'. It was just like being at home in Glasgow. He was helping all to pass the time during the long monotonous miles on the bumpy, dusty track, until their final arrival at Mount Isa.

One subsequent evening, when enjoying a welcome pint in the pub of the mining camp, Jimmy heard a man call out his name. It was someone, whom he'd met in Canberra in the early days after his arrival in Australia. The name he had called out across the room was, "Jimmy, The Singing Carpenter"! A name he had already become known by in this big friendly country, as, wherever he was, he had always sung all day, while he worked.

Days were long and hard, but every Friday afternoon, the boss gave them a keg of beer to drink while relaxing by the nearby local creek. Singing contests were organised there between the different groups of trades, and Jimmy was always competitive and popular with his repertoire of Scottish songs. It became a short, fun-filled interlude, before they had to return to work later.

He joined the local Scottish Society in the town and enjoyed the camaraderie with his own folk from his Scottish homeland. They held Saturday evening socials and dances, with everyone bringing a plate of food and all contributing to the entertainment.

One special evening, he looked across the crowded room, when, in the distance, his eye caught sight of a beautiful girl. He later discovered her name was Heather Campbell, a girl with a Scottish heritage, whose father was one of the workers at the mines. Of course, she was destined to be his future wife.

They met and danced, and had an enjoyable evening together. The next day, Heather cycled the two miles to the workers' camp, where Jimmy lived, to invite him home to have dinner with her family. From then on, they were inseparable, and her family became his. The rest of their love story is written in the pages that follow.

Of course, Jimmy still had many memories of his first wife, Lucy. He remembered Lucy's words to him, when she had last been ill, to "find a wife who could run". Now, six years on, with a new life in a new world, it would be time for him to have new beginnings.

Jimmy and Heather were a good match, as both had lost their first spouses, with Heather, as a young wife, having lost a soldier husband. A wedding was planned, but not before Jimmy had built the first of many homes he would build for them in the future.

At first, the mine-workers had mostly lived in tented homes or roughly-built shacks, made from tin and scraps of old wood. Jimmy had been employed by the company to build 'tent houses' for them. These consisted of a wooden slatted frame with canvas sides, consisting of three rooms with canvas walls, completed with a raised wooden floor, with perhaps a private covered utility and washing veranda on one side.

After months, maybe years, of living in makeshift huts or tents, they regarded these new homes as heaven to live in. Today, in 2017, these 'Mineworkers' Tented Houses' he helped to build, are protected on the Australian Heritage List.

Pioneer Hut photographed at Herberton Historic Village, 2016

Jimmy built a tented home for Heather's parents, but customised it with his skills, giving it wooden first-floor walls and ceilings, so they were able to have a tented canvas upper room for sleeping. He then made them a table and benches to sit on, much to the envy of many others.

As there were no shops to buy furniture in basic outback mining towns, people made tables and stools out of old salvaged dynamite boxes and any scraps they could find.

All this extra building work for the family had, of course, to be done in his spare time. Having duly displayed his skills to his future in-laws, Jimmy then turned his hand to the building of a home for his future bride. Once he had built them a small wooden bungalow, it was then time for the couple to be married.

The wedding took place in December 1954, and Jimmy and Heather were married with great Scottish-style celebrations. Jimmy was magnificently kilted in his Pipe Major's uniform, and his best man, Walter Irvine was also in his finery, as both of them were members of the successful Mount Isa Pipe Band. To cap it all, Jimmy ended the day's celebrations by singing to his new wife Robbie Burns's romantic song, 'My Love is Like a Red, Red Rose'.

Jimmy and Heather's wedding day, 1954
Best man Wally Irvine and his wife, Heather as bridesmaid

Wally Irvine was an old Navy pal of Jimmy's – he had been chief stoker on HMS Pheasant. When on shore leave in Brisbane at the end of the war, he had met, fallen in love with, and married a local girl, also called Heather. When the war ended, he had received permission to be demobbed in Australia, thus never needing to return home to Britain.

He, too, had gone up to Mount Isa for work and, one day, he bumped into Jimmy. It had been eight years, since Jimmy had left HMS Pheasant at Base Manus, and so, both were thrilled to see a familiar face. Happily, from then on, the two couples were to become life-long friends.

As a gift to Wally and his wife, Jimmy had made them a table and a set of stools from a piece of milky pine he had managed to obtain. Wally painted them a smart, bright red and they proudly used them in their kitchen for many years. Jimmy recalls that, over fifty years later, he and Heather went to Mount Isa for a visit to Wally and his wife, Heather, for her eightieth birthday, only to see that Jimmy's red furniture was still being used as barbecue furniture by their sons. A fitting tribute to Jimmy's first-class joinery skills.

Happy years came and went. A son, Malcolm was born in September 1955 and, in October 1957, the family was complete with the arrival of Christine, specially named after his baby sister, who had died very young.

Jimmy and Malcolm, 1955

Heather, Malcolm and Granny (Heather's mum) holding Christine,1957

Jimmy and his new wife, Heather, created a whole new business out of his part-time house-building, which he combined with working in the mine. Essentially, he built new houses in his spare time, only sleeping a few hours a night, doing a day shift at the mine, followed by a quick meal at home. He then built his houses until two in the morning, went home to sleep, and got up at seven, in order to resume his day's work again. He was working tremendously hard to provide for his family.

He and Heather jointly planned each build they did. Heather priced and bought the materials, and he organised and used his carpentry skills to complete the home. They discussed ongoing issues and made joint decisions, always respecting each other's opinions. It was a method of working they used in everything they did together, always offering each other mutual support.

Brother, Frank, and May's wedding day in Dublin, 1956

Glasgow, 1958

At this time, in November 1958, to be precise, a moving little cameo of life back in Glasgow was to be played out. Jimmy's brother, Frank, now married to his cousin, May Wogan, had a daughter, Angeleen, and was living in a tenement in Cavendish Street. One Saturday, Frank and May, together with his father and mother, John and Sarah Hughes, went into Biggar's music shop in Sauchiehall Street, where they all recorded Christmas greetings to James (Jimmy) and family. The vinyl record was then posted to him in Australia.

John Hughes then wrote about it to his daughter, Sally Goad, in Stretham, saying, "James will get such a surprise to hear our voices after so long away. It is nine years exactly on Monday, since he left us to go to Australia!"

Reading this letter fifty-five years later, which was kept so safely by my late mother-in-law, Sally, was a very moving experience. These precious memories the family had kept of James, their dear son and brother, who was always in their thoughts.

Now Back to Australia

When their first house was built, they sold it on for £2,000 and used the surplus money to buy wood and materials for the next build. With their set working routines, over the years, Jimmy and Heather continued to build new homes for themselves. Their last and fourth build was their biggest and finest, with French doors onto a patio of stone paving, all surrounded by wrought iron railings. This fine house was painted yellow and white with a smart red roof, a home to be proud of.

When Heather's mother first saw it, she said admiringly, that it was as fine as a doctor's house. For, it was known that doctors always had the finest houses in outback towns.

Jimmy had got a name for himself as a bespoke carpenter, as someone who would only work from architect drawn plans, so that people would know exactly what to expect. He was offered constant work, as skilled trained carpenters were scarce in the outback, and, consequently, he ultimately ended up leaving the Isa Mine Company and working for himself.

They had many happy years living in Mount Isa – good times with friends, travelling and competing in Pipe Band contests, and doing very well indeed, with their building business. There were also visits to the open-air canvas-roofed cinema, everyone seated on canvas chairs, watching films imported from the old country.

Jimmy could remember Heather's favourite, they had seen it many times, and it was the Scottish story of 'Wee Geordie', with Bill Travers in the leading role. Jimmy then proceeded to tell us the story, sixty years later, accompanied by great hoots of laughter, and provoking laughter all round! These had been happy days, never to be forgotten! He said, it is sometimes still repeated on television in Australia.

The following photographs were sent to, and kept by, Jimmy's sister, Sally. Jimmy wrote on the reverse of these photographs that he was proudly playing for his new Queen Elizabeth II, on her coronation tour.

Pipe band leaving Mt. Isa for Townsville during 1950s royal visit

Pipe band at Brisbane showground in 1960s – won again!

In 1964, there was a big union strike at the Mount Isa Mine Company, in a battle for workers' rights. It made the national headlines in the newspapers and turned into an eight-month 'lockout' by the mining company, causing much hardship and trouble for all the community. Jimmy and Heather decided it was the right time to sell up and move to Brisbane, where

Heather had been born and brought up, as her parents had previously returned there.

Their last big house in Mount Isa was sold for a substantial £7,000, and bought by the mine company owner. When Jimmy's daughter, Christine, and her husband, Billy, returned to Mount Isa for a holiday, they saw it had since been turned into a motel, another tribute to Jimmy's excellent carpentry and building skills.

Over the years, Jimmy and Heather had run a very successful building business. A measure of this is that, when they moved to Brisbane, they bought a block of four flats on Prince Edward's Parade at Red Cliff beach, the north end of the city. This was a beautiful part of the coastline, now known as Millionaires' Row, where the children could run straight out of their house onto the beach, and play and swim safely.

Jimmy and Heather proceeded as they had in Mount Isa, by buying a piece of land behind the local hospital and building more houses, but, this time, he built four small, two-bedroomed bungalows, which sold well. When visiting him in 2016, I took the following photographs; all four homes are still there today and look well cared for.

Jimmy also decided to obtain his taxi driver's licence for Brisbane and learned the map of the streets of Brisbane parrot-fashion from a book. He passed with 98%. The examiner said to him that he had even named roads that weren't there any more. It must certainly have been a very old book!

Sadly, at this time, Heather became very ill and had to have an operation and chemotherapy, and so, she needed a lot of after care. It was 1966 and, at this very stressful time for them, the government had decided to change the currency from the English £ to the Australian $. This revaluation of the currency caused an economic recession, affecting the price and saleability of land and houses.

Jimmy and Paddy, in front of site of old home at
Red Cliff Beach Road, Brisbane, 2016

One of Jimmy's builds in Anzac Street, Brisbane, 2016

As a result, the family decided to have another new beginning, and to go away on a long holiday. They bought a caravan and packed in it all their belongings. Jimmy once again boxed up his precious carpentry tools, and the little family headed back to the north of Queensland, to explore and enjoy the territory they knew. Much to the pleasure of Malcolm, now 11 years old, as, when he first came to live in Brisbane, he had been very homesick, because he had missed the freedom of his life in the outback.

They were camping by the famous Devil's Marbles, the gigantic, prehistoric boulders which had balanced precariously together, defying gravity, for thousands of years. When taking the photograph of them, shown below, Jimmy had written on the back that he wished he had taken the motor caravan alongside the rocks, as that would have helped to give an idea of their size. The rocks were, and still are, of great cultural and spiritual significance to the original First nations peoples.

The Devil's Marbles

The Devil's Marbles are located not far from the famous Stuart Highway, about 250 miles north of Alice Springs, and well over 650 miles south of Darwin, the capital of Northern Territory. So, Jimmy had brought his family some 1,500 miles west of Brisbane, to an area about 260 miles south of Daly Waters, where he had first settled. Alice Springs, shown on the photograph, was a mere 250 miles further south, with the outback spreading for hundreds of miles in all directions.

Near the Devil's Marbles

One day, Jimmy was approached by a road building contractor in the area. Knowing Jimmy was a carpenter and builder, he asked him, if he could put in road culverts, as he was preparing the tracks ready for later bitumen road surfacing. As Jimmy was able to read and work from plans, he agreed to help.

The work was about forty miles further north, up at Tennant Creek, which was then, a small, but productive gold-mining town. So, the family spent a few months camping there, with Jimmy working hard, and Heather teaching Malcolm and Christine each day. The children also had plenty of freedom to roam, always accompanied by their beloved puppy, Blue Dog. All looked back on the time at Tennant Creek with great pleasure.

In particular, one memory always springs to mind in the Hughes family: One day there was a big fire at the workers' base camp, and everyone immediately had to leave. So, quickly packing up their caravan, they decided to take a short holiday, and drive all of 625 miles north to spend some time in Darwin and to visit Heather's brother there, and to see where Jimmy had been on leave from his ship HMS Pheasant during WWII.

While working in the area of Tennant Creek, Jimmy and Heather had become friendly with the Chambers family, the owners of the nearby Renner Springs Roadhouse. The Chambers had offered them a year's lease to run the Roadhouse, while Mr Chambers took time out to build himself a new home. Heather's health had by then improved, and they both fancied giving the running of the Roadhouse a go, and so, they agreed to start this new venture, when they returned from their holiday in Darwin.

Malcolm and Christine were 12 and 10 years old at this time, and began having their daily schooling with the Chambers children, who had a governess. This left Jimmy and Heather free to learn all the skills of running an outback roadhouse.

At that time, Jimmy bought Malcolm a horse, a saddle and tack, so that he could spend his summer holiday of 1967 at the stock camp of his friend Wally Atkinson, who managed the Helen Springs Cattle Station. This was a bullock fattening station of a million acres, with thousands of head of cattle.

The herds wandered freely on the great, dusty plain, growing fat with the coarse, spiny leaves of the spinifex grass, grazing on the indigenous plants, and finding water from the creeks and small billabongs. When it was the season to muster them back to the station, drovers would be out for six weeks on round-up to bring them back, eating and sleeping out under the starry skies and, if caught in a tropical storm, they then slept under the cover of their 'swag' or bedroll.

Malcolm wrote a very interesting account of his school holiday experiences at Helen Springs, detailing the joys and hardships of being out in the bush and in the outback, which he has kindly allowed me to use in its entirety.

"Mustering in the Outback, 1967"

By Malcolm Hughes

When we were living at Renner Springs Roadhouse, I was about 12 years old.

Mum and Dad were friends with the Cattle Station Manager, Wally Atkinson, and I ended up in the stock camp for the school holidays.

The stock camp was very basic, in those days there was no truck or 4x4 to carry camp gear, so we had to 'Pack Horse' everything needed for a week at least, this included food, swags, tools and cooking gear. There was no refrigeration, our meat was salted and the only vegetables were a few spuds, onions and, maybe, a few old carrots.

The Station Manager had a Land Rover and would come and check up on us, bringing provisions, mail and news!

This Mustering went on for months. It is when all the cattle from the area are brought into the yards, where the youngest cattle are branded and earmarked etc. At this time, there was a drive to test all cattle for Bovine Disease, Brucellosis, I think it was called!

Most of the time, it was fairly mundane, as a kid I got the shit jobs, in the dust, at the tail of the Mob (cattle). In the dust, at the back of the yards, carrying wood and water for the Cook (The Hot and Brown expert). The best part for me was the riding, I spent a few school holidays there, and it was only on my 2nd stint there I actually got 'Paid!'

On some parts of the Station, it was very remote, miles from anywhere, and this little story happened about 100 miles east of Mount Stuart Highway. On the boundary fence with Eva Downs Station, on this day, we were to clean 'Muster' off the fence, and bring them only about 10 miles to where our camp was.

The other blokes had their area to 'Muster' and we were all going to meet before dark, as it was turning out it was a long day. I had found quite a few cattle and was having a bit of trouble keeping these wild cattle as a mob, and keeping going in the general direction, while adding more stock, and keeping the runners back in the mob. 'Hard Riding all Day'

As the day wore on, the cattle calmed down a bit, and I was able to keep them moving on. It was later in the afternoon, after lunch 'on the run', which was a lump of salt meat and another lump of 'damper' (Australian bush-bread). After lunch, I was chased by a Tiger Snake. I don't know why it was so aggressive, but I didn't hang around to find out, and it was then I thought how lucky I was, that my horse wasn't bitten; it would have killed him and I had a long way to go.

As it turned out, I managed to get the cattle where they were supposed to be, but, it was late at night, when I got to camp. Only to find no one else was there! Thinking to myself, "These blokes work late!" Anyway, I stoked up the fire, and found some more salt meat and cut a lump off and chewed away. About an hour later, the other blokes turned up, saying they had been out looking for me, thinking I was lost. This was the rule of the outback!

It was later, when we were sitting around drinking tea, it was discovered that the salt meat had had a visitor during the day in the shape of a fly, and the meat I had hungrily scoffed into in the dark was not alone! Anyway, it didn't kill me.

After returning from Renner Springs, the family and school work, they just didn't have the same appeal! That was only one of the highlights of one School Holiday.

On another holiday break, returning to the Stock Camp, there were a few strange faces around. I was told the Head Stockman and one of the 'ringers', a fellow named Johnny, had had a gun fight, shooting at each other through the Cattle Yards. I don't think anyone was hit, but neither were there any more incidents. Even so, quite the 'Wild West'.

We had been out 'mustering' all day and the thousands of cattle were yarded and just milling around in the corral, which caused huge volumes of dust that could be seen for miles. It drifted like a cloud high in the sky, like a signal indicating the location of the Stock Camp. Then, thousands of cattle were loaded each night, done in the dark to keep them calmer. They were herded into two-tier trucks for their two-day journey to the Townsville slaughter house. It seemed a life of dust, work and welcome sleep.

When the season of all this hard work was completed, it was then the time everyone looked forward to, the welcome relaxation of going into the town for Race Week.

The Race Meetings and Rodeo, which took place in the nearby town of Renner Springs, were a time for the men to 'let off steam' after the long weeks out on the plains. There were travelling 'Boxing Booths' to compete and win prizes, then the 'showing- off' of their horse riding skills in the 'Rodeo Ring', and, at the end of the week, the exciting horse racing, with all the betting, drinking and, sometimes, a good fight. All with the added comfort of sleeping in a proper bed, and enjoying lots of good fresh meals – such a welcome break from constant salt beef.

* * * * *

For a teenage boy, school could never compare with the exciting and grown-up life Malcolm saw on his holiday visits to Helen Springs Station. He has proved to be an excellent story-teller, whose descriptions of life in the outback have added a dimension to our story, which would have been beyond anyone who had not had personal experience of it. So, many thanks to him for his contribution.

Back to the Family in Renner Springs, 1967

After their happy enjoyable year was up at Renner Springs, Jimmy, Heather and family went back to live at Tennant Creek. Malcolm and Christine went to school in the town, and Jimmy had been offered a job as a surface carpenter at the gold mine there. Apart from the vast Tableland pastures and the amazing scenery nearby, Tennant Creek was well-known for mining, once having possessed the third largest gold mine in Australia.

Things went well until he was needed to work below ground, which he didn't enjoy at all. One morning, while walking to work, he felt uneasy, and so, he just turned round and went home. He heard later, that during that day's shift, there had been a collapse in the mine and all his tools and gear he had left there from the day before were lost! Fate had certainly smiled on him that day!!

This experience made Jimmy and Heather review the future and, when they saw a roadhouse for sale by the Mount Stuart Highway, south of Renner Springs, they put in an offer and were accepted.

This hot desert centre of Australia, where they had chosen to live, with no cooling rivers, had been transformed almost a century before, when the new European settlers came and drilled artesian wells, and found water. It was the Australian Overland Telegraph Line, under construction from the 1870s, which led to the drilling of these wells in this vast area.

Deep below the surface, for thousands of years, the water had seeped through layers of porous rock, filtering out many of its contaminants. As a result, cleaner, safer drinking water was made available and, naturally, small communities and cattle stations sprang up, whose names often ended in Wells, Creek and Waters and so on. The most famous of these is Alice Springs. But, long before the settlers came, this barren land, with its unique wildlife, birds and plants had been successfully populated, for many thousands of years, by its indigenous peoples, who had managed to survive, thanks to their inherited life skills. It was there, in the distant heart of the new world of Australia, that Jimmy and Heather had decided to make their home and build their future.

The Ti Tree Roadhouse Years

Ti Tree is the nearest township to Alice Springs, which is about 120 miles south. Tennant Creek, where Jimmy and Heather had lived, was 200 miles further north. Their home from then on would be the Roadhouse – just a broken-down store, according to Jimmy – which was situated in a remote place in the hot desert centre of the outback, known by its population as 'Never, Never Land', and surrounded by endless miles of red sand.

From November to March, the average temperature was 110 degrees, dropping to around 65 degrees in the winter. But, in Jimmy's own words: "When the rainy season comes, there can be 10 inches of rain in two days, but then days of breath-taking colourful sunrises and sunsets, and, at the time of the flowering citrus trees, you would not want to live anywhere else."

Living in the heat and heart of the central desert, some 800 miles south of Darwin, never had Jimmy ever felt further from his home in Scotland. But, from 1968, this would be their happy home for many years.

All there was at Ti Tree, when they first went there, were five dwellings: the Roadhouse Pub, a police house, a post office and two other houses, with ten European residents in all. There was also a nearby government camp, where 700 aboriginal people lived.

The run-down wood- and tin-built Roadhouse Pub consisted of a bar room, a small dining-room, a kitchen and store-room, and an office, which doubled as the only bedroom. The only building made of brick was a small cold room. Finally, outside was a petrol pump they owned.

Therefore, the Pub served as a service station to the passing trade of trucks and tourists, on their way, either north to Darwin, or south to Alice Springs. Of course, the local trade came from the surrounding indigenous community and the nearby cattle stations.

In fact, Ti Tree had begun its life in 1919, as part of the construction of the Overland Telegraph Line, when a well had been sunk there, producing good, sweet water. And so, by World War II, it became ideal as a 'fuel and feed' overnight stop for war-time troops going north to Darwin.

Therefore, Jimmy and Heather could see the potential there at Ti Tree, but, after the considerable decline in the 1930s, and especially since the end of World War II, there were many improvements to be made. The very first thing he did was to build a new block of toilets, which he considered a top priority.

By that time, Malcolm and Christine were teenagers and of the age to go away to boarding school, 120 miles away at Alice Springs. However, they could come home one weekend a month and had long school holidays, which they sometimes spent at the homes of their friends. Some weekends, they would bring home to stay at Ti Tree schoolmates, who were not fortunate enough to be able to visit their own parents. Some of these friends might, perhaps, see their parents only once or twice a year, as the latter could be living long distances away, working on remote cattle stations.

After Malcolm's experiences of mustering in the outback, not surprisingly, he did not cope well with the restrictions of boarding school. He missed the general freedom of life in the bush. After one incident at school, he ran away and went on 'walkabout' with his friends. At home, his playmates were the Aboriginal children. He learnt their survival ways in the desert, understood their culture and the language, and he was able to speak some of the words himself. Jimmy had an understanding of how Malcolm felt and, in any case, knew where he was by means of the local Aboriginal grapevine, and so, it all worked out OK.

Before long, Jimmy had improved the heating and lighting, as well as the water supply. Gone were the kerosene-run fridges and the Tilly lamps of the past, to be replaced with electricity produce by generators. As for the water supplies, he replaced the windmill pump he had installed, with pumps driven by generators.

This meant piped running water, which could then be heated by electricity. It compared very favourably indeed with the old system of heating hot water for a bath or shower on a contraption called a water donkey. This had consisted, essentially, of two 44-gallon drums, one on top of the other. The bottom one was filled with cold water, which was heated by a fire beneath it. The boiling water then rose into the top drum, which had a tap in it to extract the hot water.

This more primitive technology worked well enough in its day, making bathing and washing possible. Such as it was, it had been a blessing in that hot desert climate. In many such ways, Jimmy's inventiveness would take the Roadhouse into the modern era.

Painting of Ti Tree Wells Roadhouse

Over the first years, Jimmy gradually built a manager's house, and a tourist caravan park with toilets and swimming pool. He then added four motel rooms with luxury facilities, a new Roadhouse Restaurant and a new General Store. Before long, they were also running the Telephone Exchange and local Post Office.

Within a few, short years, Jimmy and Heather had transformed the Ti Tree Roadhouse and, with the increase in tourism of the 1970s, they were running a very successful business. Heather stocked painted plates, tea towels and other gifts in the store, for the visitors to take back home as souvenirs of their stay.

On top of everything else, Jimmy had three buses running in the territory, taking and fetching the native children to government schools each day: altogether, about a forty-mile round trip.

Jimmy and Heather had strong links, in fact, with the local aboriginal people. They accepted their different way of thinking and living, and were adaptable when they would suddenly disappear for days, on what was known as 'walkabout'.

Jimmy recalls that, at certain significant times for them in their culture, they could be heard out in the bush, along with the sounds of their clicking sticks and the sonorous musical tunes of their didgeridoos, playing at their secret gatherings of tribal customs. They could easily feed themselves off the land, find water from plants and trees, and they were amazing bush trackers and hunters. It was learnt, never to mention a deceased member of their family and, if one of them had done something against the tribal law, the elder could point a bone at him and he would disappear into the bush, never to be seen again.

The local aboriginal people have retained their customs of an ancient civilisation. It is a culture which, in the past, was not understood, but the government today is doing so much more to help it, and them, to survive with dignity. In the past, their main downfall was caused by liquor, which blighted many lives, but, today, their art is treasured and widely sought after, and their stories of 'Dreamtime' are being preserved for the future.

Jimmy and Heather employed several, and found them to be hard workers, who soon learnt what was expected of them.

Heather employed the girls to help her in the kitchen and the laundry. Each morning, when they arrived for work, she first gave them a cooked breakfast and a shower, and then a clean uniform for working in. She fed them daily at work and sent them back home in the evening in their own freshly laundered clothes, to the nearby government camp where they lived.

Each family had its own corrugated tin hut, locally known as a 'humpy', and they did their cooking on fire pits outside. According to Jimmy, they all seemed to be contented with this way of life. He and Heather liked and trusted these indigenous peoples, who were faithful in their friendship, and coexisted happily with them.

When their babies were due, the women looked to Heather to care for them, and they would walk from miles around to be with her at this time. Many times, in the evening, she would happily bring down to the bar a newborn baby, cuddled in her arms showing it round to all present, as proudly as if it had been her own.

The uneducated, but quick-witted, bushmen learnt quickly by watching Jimmy, and in time, Billy Manyana could be trusted to keep all the engines serviced and running smoothly at the Roadhouse and he also learnt the elements of carpentry and many other useful skills. Jimmy was very pleased with Billy's work and, on one occasion, as a sort of bonus, Jimmy gave him one of the prized Scottish tweed suits he still had in his possession.

The tourist buses came through on their way to Darwin and, after leaving Ti Tree, they would stop to view the official geographical centre of Australia at Central Mount Stuart, 12 miles north on the highway. Its popularity had meant that it had started to get untidy with litter, as the tourists' discarded papers had blown miles in the wind and got caught on the wire fences. With Ti Tree being the closest settlement, the local government officer contacted Jimmy to ask if he could send someone to clear the fences regularly.

This job of clearing the fences fell to Jimmy's son, Malcolm, and his old school-friend from Alice Springs, Billy McKerlie. By then, the children had finished school and used to help out in all sorts of ways; Christine used to help Heather in both the shop and the restaurant. For, as we have seen, the Hughes's business in Ti Tree had expanded very rapidly in their first six or seven years there. So much so, it seems, that his fame had spread to his home city of Glasgow.

Tourist Memento for Sale in their Store

Busking in Kurunda, 2016

'Glasgow Man's Thrilling Life in The Outback'

In March 1975, the Hughes family in Glasgow had been delighted to read this headline in their local *Sunday Post*, accompanied by a full page spread and a photograph of their own James Hughes. By some device, Jimmy's brother, Frank, must have contacted the press, we are forced to surmise. He would probably have passed the copy of the *Sunday Post* on to his sister, Sally Goad, in Stretham, as they had kept close contact over the years. She had then tucked it away in a drawer, having written 'Brother James' on the front, for us to find it twenty-five years later.

In the paper, therefore, Jimmy Hughes's family – including his cousin, Irene, and his brother, Frank – were proud to read an interview with Jimmy Hughes by the *Post's* roving reporter for their weekly feature, called 'The Honest Truth'. It promised all its readers to take them "12,000 miles away from it all, where Scots find themselves in some far-flung spots, but none more so than Jimmy Hughes".

The article then went on as follows: He is the nearest inhabitant to Central Mount Stuart, the geographical centre of Australia. It's the most desolate area of the Outback. Yet Jimmy and his wife, Heather, their son and daughter, have found success and happiness there, as his answers to our questions reveal. Quoted below are extracts from the long interview, in order to give readers an idea of the questions and, above all, the special flavour of Jimmy's replies:

What's your job?

I run an oasis! Well, what we call a bush pub. Simply called a tank and tummy station when I took it over. We are the last stop on the 1,000-mile road between Darwin and Alice Springs.

What's the road like? The Track? There isn't another road in the world like it, a bitumen and gravel strip through hundreds of murderous miles in any direction.

There are hazards you'd never dream of. Kangaroos are a menace. If a big boomer bounces into you, it's like hitting a brick wall.

What sort of other wildlife do you have around you?

Snakes, bush turkeys, dingoes, rabbits and gonnas, a long greenish lizard, which can sit up on its hind legs, to be easily speared by the local natives, then they cook him over an open fire as a great delicacy. The birds are so beautiful, if they are disturbed from the ghost gum or eucalyptus trees, they fill the sky with a magical mosaic of colour.

What's your closest link with home?

I've an electric piano organ, my pride and joy. I'll greet a coach-load of tourists with a selection of Scottish melodies. My pipes are on loan to the Alice Springs pipe band. It's so hot they have to keep them in the hotel fridge to keep the reeds moist.

What's the big social event of the year?

Hogmanay, of course, when we have open house for any traveller on The Track.

Also, when the circus comes to town! People come from up to 200 miles away to pack the big top. You should have seen the reaction of my regulars, when the elephant got out of hand and gate-crashed my bar. Some of the regulars haven't stopped running!!

Scots seem to adapt to life in Australia better than other nationalities. Why?

I asked a thoroughbred Aussie that question. He said, "Scots are likeable blokes, and fair dinkum and not afraid of hard work."

Researching and writing this I am sure that is true. It might be thousands of miles from true civilization, but life never seems dull!

The Sunday Post, March 9, 1975. 9

The Honest Truth Takes You 12,000 Miles Away From It All

Glasgow Man's Thrilling Life In The Outback

SCOTS find themselves in some far-flung spots. None more so than Jimmy Hughes.

He's the nearest inhabitant to Central Mount Stuart, the geographical centre of Australia.

It's the most desolate area of the Outback. Yet Jimmy and his wife, Heather, son and daughter have found success and happiness there, as his answers reveal—

WHAT'S your background?

Born in Glasgow at 159 Pollokshaws Road. My first job was messenger boy for the Netherlee Co-Op.

I joined the Navy in 1942 and served in Australian waters. Darwin and the rugged Northern Territory aroused my pioneering spirits. I always vowed to come back.

WHAT'S it like where you live?

Ti Tree Wells is 120 miles north of Alice Springs. We boast a population of 10 Europeans and about 30 aboriginals. You can never be sure of the aborigines, because they still go walk-about at any time.

There's a cattle station 12 miles from us. Remember the stations around here can be as big as Argyllshire. The only way the ranch-hands can check the perimeter fences is on a motor-bike.

By the way, there's a metal box on top of Mount Stuart. After you print this, I'll climb to the top and leave a copy of "The Sunday Post" there. At 2770 feet, you'll then be top paper in the Outback!

WHAT'S your job?

I run an oasis! Well, what we call a bush pub. It was simply a tank 'o' tummy station when I took it over—a place to fill up yourself and your car. I've motel and caravan park with luxury facilities. We're the last stop on the 1000-mile road between Darwin and Alice Springs.

WHAT sort of weather do you experience?

Summer, November to March, the average is about 110. It really burns, believe me. But when you arrive at Ti Tree, and the scent of citrus fruits wafts your way,

pital for further treatment, with the snake as a sample. I lived. The snake was dead on arrival. So much for the quality of my blood!

HOW vital is the Flying Doctor service?

It can be a life-saver. It covers two million square miles — that's 66 times the size of Scotland. Each subscriber has a two-way radio link-up with base. We also have a medical chest where every item from calamine lotion to spare corks is numbered and individually listed. Then we've a chart with various parts of the body marked off, rather like the way a butcher displays cuts of meat. So for a pain in C3, say, you take two teaspoonsfuls of B77.

WHAT'S the road between Darwin and Alice like?

The Track? There isn't another road like it in the

here. I've seen some right rough-houses, but all good fun.

DO you come across many other Scots?

They're everywhere. I just about fell away the morning a swagman wandered in wearing tatty tartan trews. Thirty years in Australia and he still had a Govan accent. There's a whole colony of Scots in Alice, including wee

and not afraid of hard work."

WHAT'S your closest link with home?

I've an electric piano organ, my pride and joy. I'll greet a coach-load of tourists with a selection of Harry Lauder melodies.

My pipes are on loan just now to the Alice Springs pipe band. It's so hot, they've to be kept in a hotel

● On the right, the Darwin-Alice Springs "track" that runs for 1000 miles through the Bush. Not far from Jimmy Hughes' place, the road runs through Edinburgh Creek—but there's nothing there!

It's Still A Mystery In Pitlochry

FOR years, Skipper has been familiar to visitors at Pitlochry. He lived in a little tent down by the river.

No one knew where he came from. He kept himself to himself.

But despite living rough, he was always as smart and clean as the next. Many local people believed Skipper was an ex-Guardsman.

He never borrowed money. No one knows how he made a living.

But progress has caught up with Skipper. Road works were planned across his camp site.

He's moved into an old folk's home in Perthshire.

And in Pitlochry it's still a mystery who he was and where he came from.

The Sunday Post, Glasgow, March 9th, 1975.
Image and quotes courtesy D C Thomson

Brother Frank with daughters, Bride Angeleen, and two bridesmaids, twin sisters, Sarah (Sally) and Teresa (Terry).

What's revealed in this interview is a particular Scotsman who has worked hard to gain acceptance in Australia, where his energy and his personality have been much appreciated. When asked, a 'thoroughbred' Aussie had said that Scots were 'fair dinkum' and not afraid of hard work. We can well believe it. it was a life full of incident, too, it seems, and a tale told by Jimmy with characteristic gusto.

Little wonder, therefore, that for his brother, Frank, and his sister, Sally, the *Sunday Post* interview was such a treasured item, as it brought them closer again to the brother they had not seen for 25 years. For Jimmy's sister, Sally, in particular, it was a precious memory to accompany the photograph she always kept on display on her polished sideboard – the one of her dear brother, Jimmy, and his wife, Heather, on their wedding day in 1954.

Back to the Hughes of Australia

After that surprise visit to the Glasgow of Jimmy's birth, we can now return to his family in the new world of Australia. Jimmy and Heather's family life was moving on. In 1975, Malcolm married Jenny from Sydney. Their son, Damian, was born the following year, the same year that Jimmy's daughter, Christine, married Billy McKerlie, to the great delight of her parents.

Billy, whom they knew well, of course, had been back in Alice Springs doing a boilermaker's apprenticeship. He and Christine soon had a son, Donald, joined by a daughter, Heather, in 1979. Jimmy and Heather were, therefore, proud grandparents, who loved to have all their family to stay at Ti Tree for holidays.

Heather loved the sport of fishing and they would take trips whenever they could. Their first car was an Austin A40, which Heather always made sure was carefully packed up with a plentiful supply of both petrol and water. One always had to consider first one's ultimate survival in this hot, dry, dusty, barren climate!!

She would then pack the 'Tucker Box' full of good food, but, most importantly, a small 'Coolgardie Safe', which was a hessian covered box frame with muslin strips hanging over the sides. These rested in a base filled with water, so that the wet muslin kept the box damp and cool, enabling the food, butter and milk to stay fresh. Lastly, not forgetting the folding grill for frying and toasting the meats and the bread in the camp-fire. Although in the past, in Jimmy's early days of travelling, he had been known to produce a good meal, cooked on a hot flat river stone, or even an old shovel in the fire!

All this meticulous care was taken for an outback picnic feast, when they went away in search of some welcome family relaxation. To this day, Jimmy remembers many happy days, spent on trips like this.

In the late 70s, Heather and Christine went to Daintree on the north-east coastal region of Queensland for a holiday. Heather so fell in love with the area, that she convinced Jimmy it was time they should sell up and live there. She had also found a house she liked, and Jimmy, always open to new ideas, happily took a flight there, to see what Heather had set her heart on.

In 1980, Jimmy was turning 56 and had started thinking about the future and his life. He had always hoped at one time to take Heather for a visit back home to Scotland, but when the time seemed right, he found they didn't have a passport and the decisive moment passed them by.

Also, when he left Scotland, he had always dreamed one day of bringing his mother out to Australia. The years of the 50s and 60s had all the difficulties of travelling and communication with the other side of the world, all of which was so primitive then, compared to the ease of today's technology. A final factor was his mother's subsequent poor health, and so, sadly, it had never happened.

Recently, he had had thoughts on retirement, as he had been constantly focused on working, since he had first landed in 1949. On the other hand, Jimmy could also see that a good future could be had in a spot nearer the coast.

The move to the coast near Daintree

For all of these reasons, for Jimmy and Heather, it was time for another new beginning and so they decided to lease Ti Tree Roadhouse for a while, and moved to start a new life living beside the great River Daintree, exchanging 'Never, Never Land' and the dry, red desert of the outback, for the lush, green, tropical rainforest environment of north-east Queensland.

But, after they had moved and become settled in the Daintree, they decided to sell the Ti Tree Roadhouse. To this day, it is still a successful stop on the Stuart Highway, owned by the big Australian company 'Gday', who run a chain of pubs and hospitality venues across the country.

They had bought 160 acres of land and a house on the north side of the Daintree River, surrounded by trees, undulating hills and green clearings. Jimmy set to and, with his carpentry skills, made the house to their liking. He also built a small boat, so they could get provisions from the nearest village of Daintree, which was across the wide river in the distance. Care had to be taken when boating on the river, as they were now in the wild, dangerous crocodile country. This little boat was still in his garden at Mareeba in 2016.

Jimmy then set to, cleared a lot of the land, put it to grass and bought a herd of cattle to graze it. Typically, he was always ready to try something new. He named this new home 'Heather Glen', as a tribute to Heather and her Campbell heritage, which he like to tease her about. What Jimmy had created for them both was a little piece of Scotland in tropical Queensland.

He found the local tropical predators a bit different from the ones he had been used to dealing with in the heat of the desert. Always having to take care not to step on a red bellied snake, having to cope with new kinds of biting insects. They had always to be aware of the sly, snapping crocodiles, when out in their little boat on the river, as, over the years, many people had disappeared and quite often there were reports of crocodiles snatching unsuspecting people from the river banks.

One night, Heather woke Jimmy, after hearing noises in the house and on investigation, Jimmy found a big black python had got in the bathroom. It was in the process of eating a basket of little kittens, and Jimmy was only able to dispatch it with great difficulty by jamming its long large body in the door. Windows and doors were carefully checked each night before going to bed after that frightening experience.

View of Heather Glen land, 2016
The roof of their white house and the jetty just visible in the trees.

After a few years, they were getting the homestead just as they wanted it, and they had teenage grandson Damian from Sydney living with them for a while. In 1985, Jimmy and Heather, as they always seemed to, saw an opportunity for a new business. Living where they did, and observing the expansion of tourism on the north coast of Queensland, they thought of starting cruise boat rides down the River Daintree.

So, Jimmy set to and designed a two-tier boat, for passengers below and a top tier for a steering cabin and 50 passengers. He then had it built at a boatyard in Cairns, about seventy-five miles to the south of them. It was to be captained by his son, Malcolm, and his new partner, Helen, for them to run. He decided to call her 'The Daintree Lady'. It was now 1986.

The Daintree Lady River Cruise Brochure

Malcolm bought a tourist bus and arranged for booking agencies along the coastal towns to sell their boat cruise tickets. Passengers would then be collected by bus in the morning, and driven up the tourist Captain Cook Highway, while Malcolm gave them a commentary on the historic coastal tour to the village of Daintree. They then transferred to 'The Daintree Lady' for a relaxing cruise down the river.

Malcolm captained and, with the benefit of his vast local knowledge and observations, gave an informative description of the wildlife. Passengers viewed the interesting flora, sleeping snakes curled high in trees, butterflies and numerous birds and, of course, they always wanted to see the legendary prehistoric crocodiles!

Sleeping Black Python (above) and Sleeping Crocodile (below)

Heather and Jimmy prepared a meal of sandwiches, cake and tea for all the tourists on their return, to complete their day out. Another successful team effort, which was to continue for many happy years.

But, Heather's health was beginning to fail. In the heat and humidity of the tropical climate of far north Queensland, she was finding it difficult to breathe, and discovered, when travelling south, visiting the Atherton Tablelands, she felt a lot better. So, Jimmy and Heather decided to leave Malcolm and Helen running 'The Daintree Lady' and go south to find a suitable new home.

After visiting several places, they finally decided on the town of Mareeba, about 65 miles due south of Daintree and less than an hour inland from Cairns. Their new house, which was chosen by Heather, was bought, because it reminded her of the one Jimmy had built for them in Mount Isa. It was a big bungalow with a traditional front veranda, situated on an acre of land at the edge of town, in Salihe Avenue.

So, in 1993, it was for them another new beginning. These were good years for the family, now all living in easy travelling distance from each other. Christine, Billy and their children, Donald and Heather, were living at the small town of Mount Molloy, some forty miles to the north.

Malcolm and Helen's son, Steven, had been born in 1990. They were to sell up and move to Mareeba, where they still are. Over the years, they have created a number of businesses: running a coffee shop, a lychee farm on the outskirts of town, a flower shop, called Floral magic and a business called Wedding Magic. Malcolm also ran a bus for school children. They, too, have followed the family tradition of hard work and enterprise.

Malcolm's son, Damian, and his wife, Debbie, were to produce Jimmy's first great grandson, Angus, in 1996. Subsequently, Heather and Jimmy loved having all the children and grandchildren around at holiday times, especially at Christmas. There are wonderful family stories told of Heather as a special grandmother. Saying how she had the amazing gift of making this such a magical time for the children, with enchanting moments, creating marvellous childhood memories, which they have all never forgotten.

Jimmy, Malcolm holding Steven, Damian, 1990

Heather loved growing plants: she owed her success to her green fingers and all-round gardening skills and had even managed to grow roses in the heart of the central desert. And so, over the years, she enjoyed creating at Mareeba a pretty flower garden and lush, green lawns with the help of Jimmy installing an electronic watering system piped underground. This was automatically timed to water plants at night, all made possible by the very high water-table found on the Atherton Tablelands.

Jimmy had a big shed built out in the garden at the back of the garage and filled it with all the carpentry tools he had collected over the years, including some of the original ones that he had brought over from Scotland in 1949. He once made all his grandchildren a facsimile Victorian rocking horse, even making and stitching the leather saddles, with each horse being painted differently by Heather.

He also did beautiful carving, and became a member of the local Wood Turners Club, attending its monthly meetings, enjoying the talk and the woodwork skills of his new friends and looking forward to the yearly trips to the Cairns show and the annual 'Turnfest' show in Brisbane. He loved competing with a

Jimmy's Workshop 2016

Examples of Jimmy's Work including the Table 2016

wider group of like-minded people and he won many trophies for his special efforts. In this way, he enjoyed an active retirement.

Heather had bought a beautiful set of rosewood furniture from a shop in Cairns. It had been imported from Hong Kong, which is why the dining room became known as the 'Hong Kong Room'. They were then living a comfortable and happy retirement in Mareeba.

Hong Kong Dining Room

At this time, in 1995, Jimmy was in the Ex-Servicemen's Club in Mareeba, when he recognised across the room an ex-sailor, who had been serving with him on HMS Pheasant. It was Roy Creffield from England, who was visiting his Australian friend, also an ex-HMS Pheasant sailor, Keith Turner, and his wife Shelia.

The Turners had also emigrated to Australia since the war, like Jimmy. Out holidaying together, they just happened to be in Mareeba that day, and they were so surprised and pleased at this coincidental meeting with Jimmy, as it was 50 years since the three of them had been on board ship together!

After a lot of war-time reminiscences of their eventful years on HMS Pheasant, Roy persuaded Jimmy to write the tale of his solo round-the-world trip back home to Scotland in 1945. He said he would take it back to England for it to be printed, as we saw earlier, in the '*Pheasant Echo*', the ship's magazine of the U49ers association, for the interest of all his old shipmates, who had not seen Jimmy, since he waved them 'goodbye' in 1946. U49 had been the number of the ship's pendant.

Latterly, Jimmy had to have a couple of stents put in his heart, but, he quickly recovered. He also had a few other skin 'ops', the consequence of living all those years in the hot desert region, caused, doctors say, by his Celtic genes and by people not being aware at that time, of the damage sun did to the skin.

Life on the Tablelands had suited them both, but then Heather's past illness re-occurred and, after months of treatment and worry, she sadly passed away in 2003 at the age of 73 years. Such a sad day for all, and her vital role at the heart of the family was to be so terribly missed, as she had always been the true partner to Jimmy in every way, through all their years of outback adventures and in their ultimate successes. For him, and for all the family, life had to begin anew without her.

Jimmy's family continued to grow. His grand-daughter, Heather was to have two children, Trey and Ekko: and Malcolm's son, Steven, married Stephanie, and they gave Jimmy two great grand-daughters, Amelia and Poppy Dawn.

Jimmy was still to have Malcolm and Helen living nearby, in Mareeba, as well as Christine and Billy, living only an hour away in Mount Molloy. He has also enjoyed the loving friendship of Heather's niece, Lee, who lives in Brisbane, and her cheerful phone calls continue to brighten his life to this day.

His love of carpentry and woodcarving has continued to fill his hours, as, for some time, he still enjoyed the camaraderie of his fellow enthusiasts at the monthly meetings of the local Wood Turners Club. Latterly, as his eyesight has begun to fail, with the assistance of his son, Malcolm, and his friend, Jim McConnachie, Jimmy has spent more and more time in his shed, cheerfully looking to the future, making beautiful gifts to give to all his family.

One of Jimmy's Rocking Horses

When I spoke to Uncle James in 2016, he laughingly told me that Heather had all the brains and he was just the brawn. But, of course, their success was above all due to their remarkable teamwork, believing in and caring for each other with lots of love and laughter, through almost fifty years of marriage.

I am so happy to have been able to relate aspects of their remarkable life together, and I trust that I have successfully touched on the important moments and some of the not so important moments, which they shared.

I am sure that I have created just a small cameo here, but I truly hope that my words capture the essence of two happy, loving people and depict two achieving, special lives, which still mean so much to their families today.

Jimmy and Heather on their Wedding Day, 1954

Mareeba Front View

Salihe Avenue, Mareeba. 2016
'Master of all he surveys'

Mareeba Garden, Morning and Evening Visiting Kangaroos, 2016

James Hughes, 2015

Chapter Five

Family Reunions 1949-2016

Paddy and Christine

Malcolm, Paddy and James

Family Reunions

The long-anticipated day of our trip halfway around the world had arrived.

The time had come at last to pay our respects to our Uncle Joseph, at his resting place in Happy Valley, Hong Kong. His nephew, Paddy, would at last be able to visit the grave of someone, who had been spoken of all his life by his mother, but, who had tragically died the year before he was born. Then we were to travel on to Queensland, Australia to meet our 'long-lost' Uncle James, to spend time with him and his family.

As we soared into the sky over Heathrow, London, our minds wondered about the many new experiences the next three weeks would bring. Surprisingly, the map of our journey, displayed on the screen before us, showed our flight path would be taking us into the ether above Finland, Russia and China, which was an amazing thought! We then duly reached our destination and landed safely in Hong Kong.

We were collected and taken by car to our hotel, quickly travelling through the busy streets of traffic and people, surrounded by magnificent high-rise buildings. The air was warm and the sky overcast and misty, as it was nearing the end of the tropical wet season.

We booked in at The Cosmopolitan Hotel, in the Wan Chi district, a large building, which had once been the Chinese Embassy in the days of the city's colonial history.

Our room was high on the eighteenth floor, and, when looking out at the spectacular views from our window, suddenly, there was an almighty downpour and the people could be seen running in the street below, scurrying around like little ants, carrying umbrellas in all colours of the rainbow. But, ten minutes later, it was as if it had never happened. That was our first taste of being in the tropics!

On the land behind The Cosmopolitan Hotel was the old civil cemetery, known as Happy Valley. This is a common Chinese euphemism for an area where a cemetery is placed. It was the first cemetery to be created here in 1845, not long after the island became a British Colony in 1842. Much needed, as the unforgiving tropical climate soon took many lives of the new European colonial families, now living and working here. All learning to cope with threatening diseases associated with the climate of the far east, without the relief of our modern-day medicines.

We had a bird's-eye view of the cemetery from the high-rise hotel's windows, looking down onto the vast sight of the old historic graveyard, with its expanse of Victorian and Edwardian granite and marble monuments. Some majestically standing tall by the curved paths, which wrapped themselves around the green mountainous slopes, others having fallen and broken, caused by the subsidence of the span of years. But all looking out from the island shores to the blue vista of the South China Seas.

The next morning, we were met at the hotel by Kenny Yu, the secretary of The Hong Kong Royal British Legion and Simon So of the Hong Kong Ex-servicemen's Association, both Hong Kong-born ex-soldiers of Joseph's former regiment, now called The Royal Logistics Corps. This had previously been arranged for us by Lt Col J. Knowles at the Regimental Barracks at Deepcut, England.

After introductions, we took the short walk to the cemetery, escorted by Kenny and Simon, who took us to the place where Uncle Joseph had been laid. They kindly supplied us with a beautiful memorial wreath of poppies to place on his grave.

So many thoughts ran around in our heads; we were here at last.

Joseph's Grave in Happy Valley, March 2016

Kenny and Simon then drove us to the old Lyemun Barracks to visit the grounds, where, beside the old Army Chapel, a memorial stone had been laid by Joseph's regiment many years before.

The barracks is now privately owned by the local council and is run as a Holiday Camp for locals and visitors; the chapel now serves as a gymnasium, but they had kindly arranged for special permission for us to visit. Giving us another quiet moment to think about family events of the past!

Paddy at Joseph's Memorial

Old Army Chapel at the old Lyemun Barracks, now a Holiday Camp

Then it was back to our hotel, where we said our goodbyes and thanked Kenny and Simon for the hospitality they had shown us on behalf of Uncle Joseph's regiment. At the hotel, a large basket of flowers had arrived from Uncle James and family in Australia, sent for us to lay as a tribute to his brother, Joseph.

Paddy then went to the nearby market to buy a spray of flowers, also to be placed there on behalf of our cousin, Irene. On such an emotional day, we both felt we needed more time to be in the Cemetery again, and to have a private moment where Joseph lay.

Now knowing where to go, we arrived laden with flowers, and walked the well-kept, stone-tiered, curling paths to Uncle Joseph's grave, lying in a quiet corner, situated on a slope halfway to the top. This was surrounded by lush, green plants and shrubs, which had grown over time into magnificent trees, which filled the spaces with dappled shade, giving the feeling of a woodland garden. It echoed with the sounds of birdsong in the air, creating a tranquil place of calm and sanctuary.

We then laid the flowers from our families on the grey and white marble memorial stone, engraved with the tributes from the past. We had come so many miles from Britain to visit Uncle Joseph. In such a special place, we found ourselves moved, lost in the moment, full of past family thoughts and feelings, but so glad we had come as his first family visitors for seventy years.

Family Tributes for Joseph, Happy Valley

The Australian Dream and Reunions with Long-lost Family

The next day, we were high in the sky on our way to Australia for our next big reunion. It was breakfast time, when we landed in Cairns, the weather was glorious, and it was smiles and hugs all round, when we were met by Uncle James and our cousin, Christine. We immediately felt we had known them all our lives.

Next, a hearty breakfast and lots of chatting at a café in Cairns on the esplanade, overlooking the amazingly blue coral-reefed sea. After meeting Christine's son, Donald, we were then driven by her to Uncle James's home in Mareeba, where, that evening, our cousin Malcolm, his partner Helen, and their puppy, Stormy, joined us for supper and more family bonding.

We had two wonderful weeks staying at Salihe Avenue, visiting family and friends, where we were made most welcome, wherever we went. Exploring special places; stopping off to meet Denise and Brian in their glorious home, high up in the trees of the rainforest, full of exotic, many-coloured flowers, butterflies and birds; and visiting 'The Daintree', to see where Uncle James and Heather had once lived beside this great wide river. The next day, we were welcome guests at the 'Wood Turners' Club' afternoon tea.

One day we had a spectacular train ride up to the rainforest village of Kuranda, amazingly, being photographed holding a baby koala bear at a sanctuary, then, seeing the most brilliantly coloured butterflies in their habitat, and, finally, never forgetting the scenic sky-rail ride home, high above the lush, green acres of rainforest.

Paddy loved the time spent with Uncle James in his work shed, full of so many kinds of unusual woods and full of admiration at his craftsmanship!

But, most enjoyable of all were the hours spent talking and bonding as a family. I recorded Jimmy's endless stories to help me write the present chapter about Jimmy's Australian adventures. We relaxed, talked, laughed and were suitably amazed at the richness and diversity of Uncle James's seventy-year lifetime in Australia. All too soon, it was time to say goodbye to Mareeba on the morning after a gathering of the clan. It had been a night to celebrate the 60th birthday of our cousin Christine's husband, Billy. The supper and the musical evening was in the Mount Molloy fire-station, where Billy is Fire Chief. It was great to meet all the family there, and, for us, it was a wonderful grand finale to our stay in the Tablelands. For which, a big thank-you to all the Australian Hughes family.

Christine's Husband, 'Birthday Boy' Billy McKerlie

Jimmy and Helen, by The Whitby Abbey Rock, Bribey Bay

Lesley, Kuranda Koala Sanctuary

Malcolm and Granddaughter, Amelia

Accompanied by Uncle James, we flew down to Brisbane to spend our last few days with Jimmy's niece, Lee, and her husband, Gary. Malcolm's partner, Helen, also met us there, in order to be company for Uncle James on his journey back to Mareeba.

There, we had more wonderful Australian hospitality, and had the pleasure of exploring the lovely beaches and coastline. We had a delightful lunch with Helen's brother, Graham, and his wife, Janice; we went with Lee to places where Uncle James had lived years before, which gave me even more information for my book; and there were more evenings of stories and laughter to record. Finally, we met Lee's daughter, Sasha, her husband, Dean, and their babies, Jameson and Mackenzie.

What really sticks in the mind are the relaxing evenings, after lovely dinners, spent on the veranda, which was situated high amongst the trees of the surrounding 'koala highway'. And, on those warm evenings, being visited at dusk by inquisitive kookaburras and possums. It was a truly relaxing rural sanctuary.

All too quickly, it was our last evening, when Garry cooked us kangaroo steak, and, afterwards Uncle James played Lee's old piano, singing lovely duets with Paddy. Then we all sang together on into the early hours of the morning, no-one wanting this special day to end.

A night of happiness, laughter and tears, creating memories we will never forget!

The next morning, it was the packing of cases, which were full of the wonderful collection of wood gifts, made for us by Uncle James. We had sad, tearful goodbyes, before flying homewards out of Brisbane Airport.

It had been an unforgettable visit, and a wonderful experience meeting our Australian/Scottish family. For Paddy, especially, there had been those special, happy weeks, spent with his long-lost Uncle James, and their mutual pleasure in sharing reminiscences of their Glasgow family, with both sensing the tangible link with respectively, a mother and a sister, Sally Hughes, and with their common Scottish heritage.

Garry Preparing Kangaroo Supper

Lee on the Front Veranda

An Evening of Singing and Memories!

And, on our return back home to Cambridgeshire, for both of us, there were all those memories of the Hughes family, new and old, recalled and shared with our Australian family. All are recorded in this book, in which Joseph Hughes is honoured, Irene Hughes-Finn is recognised for her dedication, and James Hughes's achievements in Australia are celebrated.

Let us not forget, that all of these new stories of the Hughes family, and the present joining of hands across the globe, owe their origin to the day in 2014, when my *Fen Farming Family* – the story of Paddy's Cambridgeshire family – was published and news of it spread far and wide, to be shared with all, thanks to the great, world-wide web!

Lee and Garry's Woodland 'Koala Highway' Sanctuary

Seventy-One Years On

April, 2017

After visiting Joseph's grave on the 70th anniversary commemoration, his regiment had recently decided to work in conjunction with The Soldiers Charity and the VC/GC Association, with a view to cleaning the grave and memorial and moving them from their original sites.

As Paddy and I had visited both sites in 2016, we knew it was needed, as, after so many years of weathering, discolouration and cracks had formed in the marble of both memorial and grave. Therefore, when asked, we were able to pass on our relevant thoughts to the VC/GC Association.

June, 2017

It has been decided to erect a new memorial tribute to Joseph Hughes GC in Hong Kong in a public place for all to see. The date will be fixed after all negotiations have been completed with the Chinese government, but, hopefully, to coincide with the 72nd anniversary in March 2018.

This would mean another trip for us to Hong Kong in the future, with the possibility, hopefully, of meeting Uncle James and Christine there, too. It is remarkable that, after so many years, Joseph Hughes's bravery is still being celebrated in this way. And the occasion would make a truly fitting conclusion to this story of two Hughes brothers and a cousin – a story which began, as we saw, with an account of Joseph's life and bravery. Another trip for us to Hong Kong in the future, and to hopefully meet Uncle James and Christine there too.

Hong Kong Memorial Dedication, March 22nd, 2018

New public memorial to Joseph Hughes GC. Hong Kong.

Uncle James, daughter Christine, Graham Tomms, Christopher Goad and wife Carole attending the service of dedication.

This new public memorial is placed outside the entrance to the Museum of Coastal Defence in Shau-kei-Wan, Hong Kong, by the courtesy of the present Hong Kong government. The majority of the memorial was paid for by Joseph's regiment, the Royal Logistics Corps, represented on the day by Major General David Burden, The Soldiers Charity, represented by their Chief Executive, Brigadier Robin Bacon, along with the VC and GC Association. The dedication service was also attended by The British Consul General. Members of the Hong Kong British Legion and Joseph's elder brother, Mr James Hughes, with daughter Christine, who flew in from Australia and attended this very moving memorial, along with other members of the Hughes family: relative and friend Graham Tomms and nephew Christopher Goad and his wife, Carole.

Sadly, we were unable to attend this celebrated family occasion, but Brigadier Robin Bacon of The Soldier's Charity and the Hong Kong Royal British Legion, which were chiefly responsible for the day's organisation, agreed to read a few thoughts and words of thanks from us, in our absence.

The reading

Wreath laying

Wreath laying

The memorial service

L-R: Christine and James Hughes, Chris Goad, Brigadier Robin Bacon, Carole Goad, Graham Tomms in Hong Kong, March 2018

The Hughes Tartan and Name

The marriage of Paul Hughes and Rachel McTavish
St. Brides Church, Fleet Street, London.
November 2003

Cousin Paul Hughes, the son of Irene's brother, Kenny, from Glasgow, had decided to wear a kilt on his wedding day, but, after research, he found there was not an official Hughes Clan tartan, only a privately owned one, which he was refused permission to use. Therefore, he decided to design one of his own.

Our clan Hughes, to which he belonged, was of Irish descent, so his idea of colour was to combine the green of Ireland with the blue of Scotland, with added yellow to unite his heritage.

The fabric was woven by the wool company, Kinloch Anderson of Edinburgh, and then made into the kilt by them, for Paul to wear on this happy occasion. This particular style is called a Hughes 'dress tartan'.

Hughes as a Surname

Hughes is regarded as a principal name of Ireland, meaning it is one of the original names, known since records have been kept. It may have originated in north-western counties of Ireland and has become common all over, with a concentration, it seems, in Dublin, Co. Louth and Co. Meath.

Over the centuries, as Celtic populations increased and moved on, the name Hughes was to spread throughout the areas bordering the Irish Sea. From Ireland, to Scotland and Wales they went, arriving, either as hostile invaders, or peacefully trading with their Celtic neighbours. In more recent times, as we know, they may have come in even larger numbers to north-west Wales, to south Lancashire and, of course, to Glasgow.

An early Gaelic Hughes 'sept' or clan is, apparently, O'h-Aodha, meaning Son of Hugh, living in Co Tyrone and Donegal. Another was Mac Aodha, being the McHugh clan living in Co Galway. With sub-divisions of the clans over centuries of time, some, but not all, of our Irish forebears were to adopt Hughes as a surname.

The Gaelic name Aodh may well be derived from the French Hughe, which itself originates in the Frankish Hugo, it seems. That name means 'mind', 'intelligence' and 'spirit', which seems highly appropriate for our Hughes family, especially for James Hughes and his remarkable achievements, recorded here.

More than that, the name also has the meaning of 'fire' or 'inspiration'. Coupled with this, the motto of some of the Hughes family crests is 'Not for Self but for Country'. These connections provide us, coincidentally, with a fitting ending to our story, reminding us, for the last time, that Joseph Hughes GC did, indeed, die for his country by fire, unaware, however, that he was being true to his ancient family heritage.

Hughes Family Tree

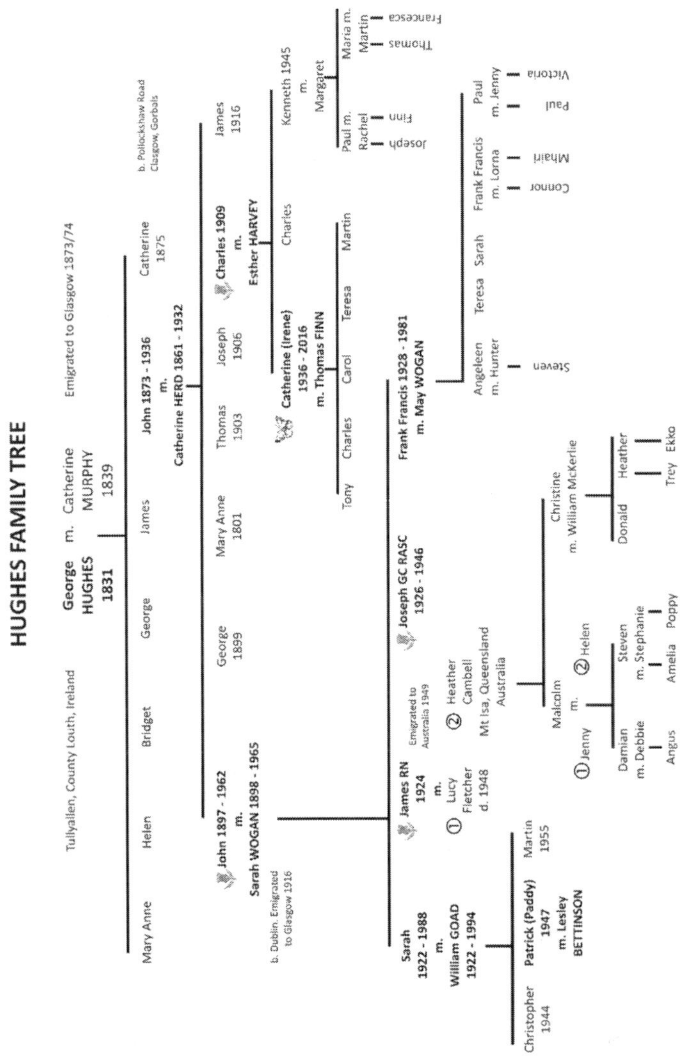

Epilogue

This book is intended, first and foremost, to be a gift to all of our Hughes families, present and future, and to the many other readers, far and wide, as an example for all those who believe and trust in the goodness of mankind. Above all, it is a story of sons and daughters of the west of Scotland, who, in their different ways, have made such a mark on the wider world.

Of Irene, our caring cousin, who so wanted this story to be told, and all she achieved in retaining Joseph's memory in Glasgow. This book is testament to her supreme doggedness and fulfils the promise made to her, after receiving her surprising 'book-angel' request a year or so before she died.

Of Uncle Joseph Hughes himself, who in 1946, at the tender age of nineteen, sacrificed his life to save others, now to be honoured yet again with a public memorial in Hong Kong in March 2018, having already rested in a grave in happy Valley Cemetery, Hong Kong for seventy-two years.

And it relates the fascinating life of Uncle James Hughes, who, as a young man in 1949, forged a new life in Australia in the Northern Territory and Queensland. Now in his nineties, he has led a life of courage, tenacity and achievement and continues to be surrounded by his own branch of the Hughes clan in Mareeba.

So, it has been a story of Irene Finn, a true Glasgow lass, who stayed at home, and of Joseph and James Hughes, her two cousins, who both left their home city to fulfil their destinies, little knowing that they would never return.

Having made a personal journey across the world in search of our two uncles, we can now say that, through this book, the Hughes family of Glasgow has become reunited and two long-lost brothers have been brought home again. Suffice it to say, in our thoughts and in our hearts, they will always remain, as much as anything else, true 'Sons of Scotland'.

Acknowledgements

In writing this book, I am indebted to the following persons:

My husband, Paddy, once again, for his support and patience.

Uncle James Hughes, for his permission to use the stories of the past, those he relayed to me during long hours of chatting, as well as his own published story, *Perils in the* Pacific.

Cousin Malcolm Hughes, for permission to use his account 'Mustering in the Outback'.

Cousin Carol McKenzie, Irene's daughter, for help with her mother's story.

Cousins Angeline McGoldrick and Frank Hughes, for help about their father, Uncle Frank.

Cousin Kenny and Margaret Hughes, for information and photographs.

Cousin Paul Hughes, for permission to use his special Hughes dress tartan.

Lt Col J. Knowles of RLC Museum, Deepcut, for his help with our visit to Hong Kong and permission to use the Regimental Badge and photographs, and also the enjoyable hospitality at RLC Deepcut Officers' mess.

Rebecca Maciejewska, Chief Executive of the Victoria and George Cross Association, for all her help with Joseph's memorial information.

Brigadier Robin Bacon, Chief Executive of The Soldiers Charity, for reading Paddy's words in his absence, at Joseph's Hong Kong memorial.

The Office of The Lord Lyon, for permission to use The Glasgow Coat of Arms.

D. C. Thompson & Co. Ltd., for permission to use *The Hornet* front cover and tribute, also quotes from the *Sunday Post*.

The *Glasgow Evening Times*, for permission to use cuttings.

The Ellis Family of Wheatfen, for permission to use the 'Fulfilment' excerpt.

Irene's friend, Elsa Beattie, for her poem 'For a Hero was He'.

Composer, Pipe Major Pat Lee, for allowing us to use the Joseph Hughes tribute pipe lament.

My brother, Dr Chris Bettinson, for proof-reading the book and giving valuable advice on the final version.

Once again, to Chris and Jane Thomas of Milton Contact Limited, Cambridge, for all the valued advice, care, patience and hard work in helping this book to become a reality.

'Fulfilment' (last two verses)

When memory's eye looks down the aisles of Time,
Let golden dreams dissolve the mists of grief:
When, in the shadow and the light, the years
Will wake and pass in beauty, one by one.

Like daffodils the young friends dance again:
Love's roses linger in the summer dusk:
Glowing the harvest where ripe wisdom dwell
And innocent December's quiet farewell.

Ted Ellis 1909-1986
Norfolk Naturalist, Author and Friend

Remembering our son, Mark. 30/10/65 - 28/12/15